Teaching Reading to Adults

to Adults

A Balanced Approach

Teaching Reading to Adults

A Balanced Approach

Grass Roots Press

EDMONTON, ALBERTA

PAT CAMPBELL

5th Printing, 2006

National Library of Canada Cataloguing in Publication Data

Campbell, Pat, 1958
Teaching reading to adults: a balanced approach / Pat Campbell.

ISBN 1-894593-18-9

    1   Reading (Adult education) I. Title.

LC5225.R4C345 2003   428'.0071'5   C2002-904158-9

Grass Roots Press gratefully acknowledges the support provided by the National Literacy Secretariat, Human Resources Development Canada.

The publisher would like to thank Houghton Mifflin Company for permission to reproduce an excerpt from *River Thieves* by Michael Crummey.

Edited by Dr. John Proctor
Book design by Lime Design Inc.
Printed and bound in Canada by Imperial Printing Ltd.

Grass Roots Press
PO Box 52192
Edmonton, Alberta
T6G 2T5

Phone toll-free: 1-888-303-3213
Fax: 1-780-413-6582
Web: www.literacyservices.com

For

the many dedicated literacy educators

with whom I have worked

over the years.

Preface

It is hard to believe that a person can graduate with a degree in elementary education and not know how to teach reading. During my degree studies, I was required to take only three credits in "language arts." Consequently, upon completing the degree, I didn't have the foggiest idea about how to teach reading.

My first classroom experience was with a group of high school students in rural Nigeria. The students, many of whom had low-literacy skills, and I struggled in our attempts to learn from one another. I vowed that when I returned home to Canada, I would pursue a graduate degree in reading. After completing a Masters Degree in 1985, I was hired to coordinate an adult literacy program. Although I felt qualified as a reading specialist, I didn't feel competent to deal with the issues and concerns of adult literacy learners. Consequently, I focused on assessment and instruction and encouraged students to access other resources for their other problems and concerns.

Gradually, I began to see that my approach to literacy was narrow in scope, and I began moving toward ways to teach reading in a participatory context. This book is directed at literacy practitioners who also want to balance instruction in "reading the word" with instruction in "reading the world."

Teaching Reading to Adults: A Balanced Approach was funded by the National Literacy Secretariat (NLS), Human Resources Development. I would like to thank Yvette Souque and Nilambri Ghai, both of whom work at the NLS, for their support and patience. The project was sponsored by the Centre for Research on Literacy at the University of Alberta. Dr. Linda Phillips, the Director of the Centre for Research on Literacy, provided me with the resources to undertake and complete this project.

Careful effort was made to ensure that educators' questions about teaching reading to adults were addressed in this book. Educators' questions were elicited through the establishment of focus groups in Halifax, Iqaluit, Regina, and Toronto. The focus groups were facilitated by the members of my advisory committee. I am very grateful to Susan Toews, Debbie Purton, Maureen Doherty, and Sheila Nunn for taking the time to organize and facilitate these focus groups. I would also like to acknowledge the educators who participated in the focus groups, as their questions kept me grounded throughout the writing process.

A special thank you goes to Dr. Grace Malicky. Grace was the first person to read the book from cover to cover. I have always valued Grace's advice, wisdom, and common sense. Over the years, Grace has served as my sounding board on various literacy projects.

I would also like to offer words of gratitude to the adult literacy and English as a Second Language educators who read the second draft of the manuscript: Susan Toews, Marg Rose, Janet Isserlis, Marg Armstrong, and Sheila Nunn. During the writing process, I asked Dr. Linda Phillips, Dr. Bob Bruinsma, and Dr. Martha Smith to read specific chapters. Each of these eight people provided a unique perspective, and their suggestions served to strengthen the content. I'd also like to thank Dan Page and Joel Maniapik for providing insight into the classroom dynamics in small northern communities.

Toward the end of the writing process, Dr. John Proctor became interested in the book and offered to edit the manuscript. I knew my work was in good hands, as John has over 40 years experience as an educator. Judith Tomlinson deserves special mention, as she was responsible for the copy editing.

Last, but certainly not least, I would like to thank my husband, Terry Barber. With Terry, I shared the high and low moments of the writing process. There were days when I couldn't seem to write a word and days when I doubted myself. Those were the days when Terry provided me with the encouragement and support I needed.

To my family, friends, and colleagues, all of whom have provided support in so many ways, thank you all.

Pat Campbell

IT'S INTERESTING—the way in which one has to balance life—because you have to know when to let go and when to pull back. The answer is never just to completely "let go" or "transgress," but neither is it to always "contain yourself" or "repress." There's always some liminal (as opposed to subliminal) space in between which is harder to inhabit because it never feels as safe as moving from one extreme to another.

hooks, B. (1994). *Outlaw culture: Resisting representations*. New York: Routledge. p. 211

T A B L E   O F   C O N T E N T S

CHAPTER ONE

Teaching Reading to Adults
A Balanced Approach

Introduction

> The International Reading Association states that there is no single method or single combination of methods that can successfully teach all children to read. Therefore, teachers must be familiar with a wide range of methods for teaching reading and a strong knowledge of the children in their care so they can create the appropriate *balance* of methods needed for each child. (International Reading Association, 1999, *emphasis added*)

In light of currently recommended approaches for teaching young children to read, adult literacy educators are being invited to consider how balance applies to their practice. As can be seen from the position statement of the International Reading Association, balance refers primarily to the decisions made by the educator in response to the learning needs of the student(s). Such a contention implies that the educator must be aware of two things: the needs of the student(s) and the resources available for responding to those needs. For adult students, these needs usually include developing the skills, strategies, and concepts that contribute to becoming fluent readers; and examining how, when, where, and why they engage with literacy activities in their lives. Resources include instructional strategies, texts, time, venues; and the political, cultural, and social contexts in which both educator and student are situated. Thus, balance in the context of adult literacy education means that the educator responds to the individual and collective needs of the student(s) by balancing them against the available resources. This book sets out the ways that educators may work collaboratively with students to identify their needs, and it suggests resources that facilitate responsive, balanced reading instruction in a **participatory**[1] context.

Aspects of Balance

IN THE FIELD OF ELEMENTARY EDUCATION, the term "balance" usually refers to the "how" of teaching reading—the methodology. Elementary teachers have available multiple ways to incorporate balance into how they teach, what they teach, and why they teach. In recognition of students' different capabilities, they integrate comprehension and word recognition strategies into their daily lessons. While teaching strategies, they may alternate between **deductive** and **inductive** instruction, **incidental** and **systematic** skills instruction, and **isolated** and **contextualized** skills instruction. To respect students' diversity, they incorporate multicultural texts, a variety of genres, and different communication modes into the curriculum.

In the field of adult literacy, the term "balance" operates not only within the context of methodology, but also within the broader context of reading the word *and* the world. In this context, a balanced approach addresses the sociopolitical and economic dimensions of reading, wherein lessons inside the classroom are tailored to facilitate students constructing meaning from and responding to text with a view towards making changes within their lives and communities. And who does the tailoring? This question opens up a Pandora's box, unleashing issues about power, control, decision-making, voice, silence, and resistance. A balanced approach to teaching reading addresses these issues, with the intent of promoting egalitarian social relations both inside and outside the classroom.

This chapter presents two themes prevalent throughout this book: balance between print and meaning, and balance between reading the word and the world. These themes are underwritten by a caveat: in the field of adult literacy, we need to be wary of dualistic frameworks that create boundaries between print and meaning, and between reading the word and the world. For instance, the whole language vs. phonics debate is really about focus on meaning versus focus on print. A balanced view of teaching reading to adults crosses boundaries and acknowledges that while the construction of meaning from text is of paramount importance, students need to learn strategies for word recognition. Let's begin by considering the methodology or the *how* of teaching, which is one aspect of a balanced reading program.

> ▶ In the field of adult literacy, the term "balance" operates not only within the context of methodology, but also within the broader context of reading the word and the world.

Integrating Print and Meaning

THE "GREAT DEBATE," a term coined by Jeanne Chall (1967) to describe the contentious issue of whole language vs. phonics instruction, is not restricted to the arena of elementary education. It has also become a question mark in the minds of adult literacy educators. The following questions, which were posed by a group of adult literacy educators,[2] illustrate the concern for finding the "best" approach for teaching reading to adults amid the confusion surrounding phonics instruction.

- What approach should you use? Whole language or phonics?
- Is phonics the best approach to take?
- Do we teach individual letters or sounds first?

- Do adults need to sound out the letters?
- What are the alternatives to phonics?
- How do we use phonics as part of a larger program?
- Why do some learners not "get" phonics? What do you do then?
- Learners often think that they should be going back to the basics and learning or relearning phonics. Teachers are sometimes opposed to this, thinking that it didn't work the first time, why try again?
- Do readers acquire skills in a particular order? Is there a "natural" order, such as phonics learning first, then sight words?

The debate about whole language vs. phonics can become emotional, so perhaps it is best to start by examining what is meant by the terms "whole language" and "phonics." This will lead us into examining what is meant by a balanced approach to teaching reading.

Whole Language

Whole language is a perspective that has as its central tenet the importance of constructing meaning from authentic texts and literacy activities. Whole language advocates reject the notion that students should learn to read by progressing through a linear, sequential series of skills. Goodman (1986), probably the best-known advocate of whole language, believes that whole language rests on the following principles:

- Literacy develops from whole to part, from vague to precise, from gross to fine, from highly concrete and contextualized to more abstract, from familiar contexts to unfamiliar.
- Readers construct meaning during reading. They use their prior learning and experience to make sense of the texts.
- Readers predict, select, confirm, and self-correct as they seek to make sense of print. In other words, they guess or make hypotheses about what will occur in the text. Then they monitor their own reading to see whether they guessed right or need to correct themselves to keep making sense.
- Three language systems interact in written language: the graphophonic (sound and letter patterns), the syntactic (sentence patterns), and the semantic (meanings). We can study how each one works in reading and writing, but they can't be isolated for instruction without creating non-language abstractions. All three systems operate in a pragmatic context: the practical situation in which the reading and writing is taking place.
- Risk-taking is essential. Developing readers must be encouraged to predict and guess as they try to make sense of print.
- Materials for instruction must be whole texts that are meaningful and relevant. (pp. 38-40)

Whole language educators believe that effective readers use **semantic** and **syntactic** cues to a greater extent than **graphophonic** cues when they are reading and decoding unfamiliar words (Weaver, 1994). If a student substituted the word "converted" for "coveted" in the sentence "The Americans coveted the colony and wanted B.C. to join the United States," the whole language educator's first response would probably be "Does that make sense?" rather than "Try sounding out the word." Among other things, the press, politicians, and the public have criticized proponents of whole language movement for their apparent lack of attention to phonics.

Phonics

Phonics is an instructional system founded on the premise that beginning readers identify words by relating speech sounds to letters and letter units. In the field of adult literacy, New Readers Press is widely known for workbooks that promote a phonics approach to teaching reading. *The Laubach Way to Reading*, for example, is a structured, phonics-based reading program for adults who are nonreaders or at very low reading levels. *Voyager: Reading and Writing for Today's Adults*, which is the most recent set of workbooks from New Readers Press, continues to promote the concept that phonics should be taught in a sequential fashion. The first workbook in the series, the *Voyager Foundation Book*, begins by teaching the students the alphabet. This introductory lesson is followed by 28 lessons that teach consonants, short vowel sounds, and consonant blends.

The assumptions underlying these workbooks are that:

- Phonics is the best approach for all beginning readers.
- The graphophonic system is more important than the semantic and syntactic systems.
- Phonics should be taught sequentially.
- All beginning readers should be taught the same way.

Balancing Print and Meaning

> Rather than choosing sides in the whole language vs. phonics debate, educators who advocate balance in a reading program recognize that teaching reading isn't an either-or situation where one approach is superior to another.

Rather than choosing sides in the whole language vs. phonics debate, educators who advocate balance in a reading program recognize that teaching reading isn't an either-or situation where one approach is superior to another. Educators who implement a balanced approach incorporate many of the principles of whole language, while recognizing the need for *explicit* instruction that integrates meaning and print and is tailored to students' strengths and needs. According to Michael Pressley, "balanced-literacy teachers combine the strengths of whole language and skills instruction, and in doing so, create instruction that is more than the sum of its parts" (1998, p. 1).

Rather than engaging in a debate about whether phonics should or should not be taught, educators who take a balanced approach consider when, how, how much, and under what circumstances phonics should be taught (International Reading Association, 1997). Rather than using a common program or approach for all students, a balanced reading program incorporates the need for responsive instruction. In order to determine the instructional needs of each student, educators administer authentic assessments that use a wide range of texts and tasks to assess a student's literacy development, skills, processes, strengths, and areas for development.

A balanced reading program, which integrates meaning and print, is supported by recent research that examined the word identification and comprehension strategies used by 344 adult basic education students[3] (Campbell & Malicky, 2002). In the study, adult literacy learners at *all levels* of reading development relied primarily upon either meaning-based strategies or an integrated use of meaning- and print-based strategies as they read. The adults in our study were able to use *both* print-based and knowledge-based information at early levels of reading proficiency. Overall, our results indicated the need for responsive instruction rather than a "one size fits all" program for all adults at any one level of reading proficiency.

The next section introduces the second theme—balance between reading the word and the world. This phrase describes an approach to literacy instruction in which the readers' critical understanding of text *and* context opens the door to creating knowledge that can be used to change their social realities. In this sense, literacy development is a political process and act. This theme is also explored in Chapter Six: Teaching Reading in a Participatory Context.

Reading the Word and the World

PAULO FREIRE (1968), a Brazilian educator, coined the phrase "reading the word and the world." Freire believed that:

> Reading the world always precedes reading the word, and reading the word implies continually reading the world...this movement from the word to the world is always present; even the spoken word flows from our reading of the world. In a way, however, we can go further and say that reading the word is not preceded merely by reading the world, but by a certain form of *writing* it or *rewriting* it, that is, of transforming it by means of conscious, practical work. For me, this dynamic movement is central to the literacy process. (Freire & Macedo, 1987, p. 35)

Freire emphasizes the relationship between readers' critical comprehension of the word and their knowledge of the world. Certainly, adult literacy educators are cognizant of the importance of activating and using students' background knowledge to construct meaning from text. Freire, however, is concerned about the production of knowledge and its relationship to power both within and outside of the classroom.

Although Freire's philosophy has been criticized for certain shortcomings, such as his inattention to the gendered role of literacy (Chledbowska, 1990; Weiler, 1991; Rockhill, 1988), his ideas relating to the critical relationship among literacy, culture, and society have implications for educators who wish to take a broad-based balanced approach in their practice. The following section discusses "reading the word" within the North American context, and draws upon my personal experiences as an educator within a volunteer literacy program and a women's health program.

Reading the Word in a North American Context

> We need political clarity before we can understand the political action of eradicating illiteracy in the United States or any other place. Educators who do not have political clarity can, at best, help students read the word, but they are incapable of helping them read the world. (Freire & Macedo, 1987, p. 132)

Educators who believe that reading is an educational issue tend to implement a literacy program where the focus is on reading the word—decoding words and constructing meaning from text. During the 1980s, while coordinating a large urban adult literacy program called PROSPECTS, I passionately believed that reading was an educational issue. My education as a reading specialist "trained" me to focus attention on the individual learner and her/his reading deficiencies rather than on social structures and practices that contribute to and perpetuate the cycle of "il/literacy." I was so enamoured of the "how" of reading—assessment, methodology, and remediation—that I ignored the "why" of reading—the sociopolitical dimensions. In my mind, "illiteracy" was the students' principal source of oppression rather than their gender, race, or class (Campbell, 2001).

During this six-year period, I was ensconced in a liberal-humanist model of adult education, a model that promotes learner-centred literacy programs. Since PROSPECTS strived to foster individual growth and learning, the program provided only one-to-one tutoring. According to Gaber-Katz and Watson (1991), learner-centredness means that educators:

- Listen to literacy learners and elicit stories about their lives.
- Believe that everyone can learn.
- Emphasize equality among learners, volunteers, and staff.
- Encourage learners to become involved, both in the program and in the community.
- Ensure that learning will be relevant.
- Provide a range of programming options.
- Assist learners in setting their own learning goals and measuring their own progress.
- Ensure that learners' interests and needs determine the curriculum. (p. 9)

Although PROSPECTS did not offer a range of programming options, the board and staff considered the program to be learner-centred. Since the program was learner-centred rather than teacher-directed, I sometimes described the program as "Freirian." In retrospect, I had whitewashed Paulo Freire's concepts and pedagogy, removing all traces of their political content. The term "empowerment" meant raising students' self-confidence so that they would be able to function independently in society. The term "critical consciousness" meant that students should become aware of their needs, and an individualized program should be constructed to assist the students in meeting these needs. However, for Freire, the term "conscientization" is a process whereby students think critically about the social, economic, and political structures that cause oppression, such as low wages, unemployment, racial or ethnic discrimination, and social isolation.

PROSPECTS was a successful program in that students' stated needs were met and their literacy skills improved. Yet, I gradually began to question the impact of improved literacy skills on their lives and my assumptions about the promises and power of literacy. For instance, did their gain in literacy skills have a positive impact on their employment? What about their unstated needs? Did their level of participation in the community increase? Were they more comfortable in settings where they consulted with professionals such as doctors and teachers? Were they standing up for their rights when necessary? Were they able to say no? Was their ability to navigate through systems, such as the legal system and the social services system, enhanced? Was the students' sense of social isolation being diminished? Was the program, by teaching students how to cope with their existing situation, simply preserving the status quo? Unfortunately, follow-up was difficult due to the focus on intake, the limited financial support, a transient student population, and the invasive nature of the process. After leaving PROSPECTS in 1991 to pursue a doctoral degree, I entered a transition period where I questioned the worth of my previous work with adults and sought to integrate new knowledge into practice.

Reading the World in a North American Context

In 1996, I contracted to develop a program for a women's health group in a community-based literacy and education centre. My role was to develop a participatory education program that integrated literacy development and health promotion. The curriculum, based on the women's issues and concerns, consisted of health topics that were explored during weekly two-hour workshops. In each workshop, we sought to create a safe environment where students and educators could produce knowledge and critique "legitimate" knowledge. For instance, we discussed our experiences with menopause and critiqued the medical profession's stance towards the treatment of menopause.

We began each workshop by discussing the women's personal experiences, which were then collectively explored and connected to systemic issues that affect health. What follows are two of the ways in which we attempted to connect the personal to the political (Norton & Campbell, 1998):

- In the stress workshop, we discussed how "living with poverty also adds to stress, as do experiences of sexism and other discrimination, racism, and abuse." (p. 32)
- In the anger workshop, we discussed how anger and its expression "may reflect power relations. For instance, the government has more power than an individual, so individuals often have to find other people who share a similar anger about an injustice. Then, they have to work together to promote change." (p. 79)

Throughout the program, the women were exposed to and read written text in books, magazines, flyers, and flip-chart notes. My colleague and I facilitated pre- and post-reading activities where we would discuss, interpret, and construct meaning from the text. We were not very successful in our attempts to integrate word recognition and comprehension strategies in a structured way. Part of the challenge was that the students differed in terms of their literacy levels and capabilities. It was also difficult to seize "teachable moments" where we could put the dialogue on "pause" in order to teach a reading strategy. In retrospect, "reading the world" was the focus for this program, rather than "reading the word."

Balancing the Word and the World

> While it is recognized that literacy is a socioeconomic and political issue, a balanced reading program also provides opportunities for students to read and learn specific strategies that will assist them to become better readers.

The experiences detailed above led me to explore integrated approaches to adult literacy education. In many ways, this exploration pointed to the critical need for balancing the multiple dimensions of adult literacy instruction. A balanced reading program provides opportunities for participants to collectively share, create, analyze, and act upon their knowledge and experiences, with a view towards building a just society through changing their social realities. While it is recognized that literacy is a socioeconomic and political issue, a balanced reading program also provides opportunities for students to read and learn specific strategies that will assist them to become better readers. While the reading of text can easily be integrated into a collective learning experience, the integration of reading strategies is sometimes problematic because of students' different literacy levels and capabilities. More importantly, it is sometimes inappropriate to introduce specific reading strategies, especially during and after an emotional and spirited dialogue.

I am now convinced that it is important to structure a literacy program that provides opportunities for students to move among group work, tutorials, and independent work. Group work provides opportunities for students to share experiences, identify issues, and introduce change into their lives and/or communities; tutorials are appropriate for the introduction of reading strategies that respond to the student's instructional needs; and reading independently promotes fluency.

Another critical aspect of balance in teaching reading to adults reflects the need for educators to be aware of their role. The 2Rs, resistance and responsibility, form a leitmotif within literature that discusses the educators' role. A tension that keeps bubbling to the surface is the difficulty that educators have in letting go of what they see as their *responsibilities regarding control of students' learning*. At the same time, students sometimes *resist* the opportunity to take a more active role in their own learning and decision-making. The following description captures a literacy educator's struggle for this aspect of balance[4]:

> it was difficult for students to find their own focus and decide what the focus should be...and [the instructors] probably need(ed) to provide a bit more structure. It's a constant *balancing act,* and you know, kind of, not jockeying for position, but just, you know, there are trade-offs. You can be more directive, but really listen to what students have to say too, and as you say, make suggestions but at the same time be open to what they have to say too. (Campbell, 1994, p. 117)

Deborah Morgan (2000), a literacy educator, used a journal to reflect upon her role with female adult literacy students in a writing group. In her journal, Morgan documents her struggles with striking a balance and poses these questions:

> Why aren't the women participating more when that is what they had indicated they wanted? (p. 116)

> Why am I having trouble letting go of the responsibility for facilitating the group? (p. 116)

> How do I help students trust this process when I'm not entirely sure of it myself? (p. 116)

> How do you know when someone is ready to get more involved in their own learning? (p. 126)

Kate Nonesuch (2001) led an electronic conference where literacy educators talked personally about "striking a balance and about walking a fine line in our attempts to provide leadership while leaving room for students also to lead." In this conference, Kate remarked that:

> ... (T)he issue of "getting out of the way" and relinquishing power starts with trust. Trust in the learning process; trust that I can take control and let it go; trust that I know what I am doing and that the students, when given true power over their learning, will for the most part rise to the challenge and engage in the process. (p. 7)

> ▶ **In a sense, teaching adults to read is like a dance, where educators have to listen to the music and know when to let go and pull back, when to step in and when to step aside. To perform the dance effectively, the partners must trust each other.**

In a sense, teaching adults to read is like a dance, where educators have to listen to the music and know when to let go and pull back, when to step in and when to step aside. To perform the dance effectively, the partners must trust each other.

CHAPTER SUMMARY

As you read this chapter, it may have become apparent that developing a balanced approach to reading instruction includes more than deciding which method to use. The key elements that lie at the core of a balanced approach to teaching reading are as follows:

- A balanced literacy program is built on insightful assessment and analysis of what adult students know and what they need to learn in order to become fluent readers.
- Educators are pragmatic in that they use available resources in ways that effectively respond to the student(s)' individual and collective needs.
- Educators are aware of the social, economic, cultural, and political contexts within which their instructional responses are situated.
- A balanced view of teaching reading to adults acknowledges that while the construction of meaning from text is of paramount importance, students need to learn strategies for word recognition.
- Adult literacy educators recognize that "reading the word" is always situated within a context of "reading the world." Lessons inside the classroom are tailored to help students construct meaning from text and respond to text with a view towards making changes within their lives and communities.

The extent to which you take a balanced approach to the teaching of reading is framed by your identity and the support and/or resistance that you encounter within your working environment. This means that your interpretations of balance will inevitably be situated within your unique context and circumstances. Just as identities are fluid and continually being reframed, your notion of a balanced approach to teaching reading will continually shift and change over time. In addition, your understanding of balance is underwritten by an understanding of *how* people learn to read and the contexts in which they learn most effectively; Chapter 2 is organized around this discussion. ❧

References

Au, K. H., Carroll, J. H., & Scheu, J.A. (2001). *Balanced literacy instruction: A teacher's resource book* (2nd ed.). Norwood, MA: Christopher-Gordon Publishers.

Campbell, P. (1994). *Participatory literacy practices: Having a voice, having a vote.* Unpublished doctoral dissertation, University of Toronto, Ontario.

Campbell, P. (2001). Participatory literacy practices: Exploring pedagogy. In P. Campbell & B. Burnaby (Eds.), *Participatory practices in adult education* (pp. 55-75). Mahwah, NJ: Lawrence Erlbaum Associates.

Campbell, P. & Malicky. G. (2002). The reading strategies of adult basic education students. *Adult Basic Education, 12*(1), 3-19.

Chall, J.R. (1967). *Learning to read: The great debate.* New York: McGraw-Hill.

Chlebowska, K. (1990). *Literacy for rural women in the third world.* Paris: UNESCO.

Fitzgerald, J. (1999). What is this thing called 'balance?' *Reading Teacher, 53*(2), 100-107.

Freire, P. & Macedo, D. (1987). *Literacy: Reading the word and the world.* South Hadley, MA: Bergin & Garvey Publishers.

Freppon, P.A. & Dahl, K.L. (1998). Balanced instruction: Insights and considerations. *Reading Research Quarterly, 33*(2), 240-251.

Gaber-Katz, E. & Watson, G.M. (1991). *The land that we dream of...A participatory study of community-based literacy.* Toronto, ON: OISE Press.

Goodman, K. (1986). *What's whole in whole language?* Richmond Hill, ON: Scholastic-TAB Publications.

International Reading Association. (1997, April). *The role of phonics in reading instruction. A position statement of the International Reading Association.* Newark, DE: Author.

International Reading Association. (1999, April). *Using multiple methods of beginning reading instruction. A position statement of the International Reading Association.* Retrieved September 21, 2002 from the International Reading Association Web site: http://www.reading.org/positions/begin_reading.html

Laubach, F. (1981). *The Laubach way to reading.* Syracruse, NY: New Readers Press.

Morgan, D. (2000). Changing places. A study about factors that can affect sharing the facilitator's roles in a women's writing group. In M. Norton & G. Malicky (Eds.), *Learning about participatory approaches in adult literacy education. Six research in practice studies* (pp. 105-140). Edmonton, AB: Learning at the Centre Press.

Nonesuch, K. (2001, April 23). *Getting out of the way.* An electronic conference on the e-northwest regional literacy electronic network. Literacy BC: First Class.

Norton, M. & Campbell, P. (1998). *Learning for our health: A resource for participatory literacy and health education.* Edmonton, AB: The Learning Centre Literacy Association.

Pressley, M. (1998). *Reading instruction that works: The case for balanced teaching.* New York: The Guilford Press.

Rockhill, K (1988). E-man-ci-patory literacy: An essay review of literacy: reading the word and the world. *Canadian Woman Studies, 9*(3 & 4), 113-115.

Siedow, M.D. (1999). *Voyageur: Reading and writing for today's adults. Voyaguer foundation book.* Syracuse, NY: New Readers Press.

Weaver, C. (1994). *Understanding whole language: From principles to practice* (2nd ed.). Portsmouth, NH: Heinemann.

Weaver, C. (1998). *Reconsidering a balanced approach to reading.* Urbana, IL: National Council of Teachers of English.

Weiler, K. (1991). Freire and a feminist pedagogy of difference. *Harvard Educational Review, 61*(4), 449-473.

Notes

1   Bolded terms are defined later in the text or in the Glossary.

2   In 2000, 30 adult literacy educators participated in focus groups in Halifax, Nova Scotia; Regina, Saskatchewan; Toronto, Ontario; and Iqaluit, Nunavut. The educators were tutors, coordinators of volunteer literacy programs, and college educators. Their experience as adult literacy educators ranged from 1 day to 30 years. One purpose of the focus groups was to document their questions about how an adult learns to read and how to teach reading.

3   This study will be described in further detail in Chapter Two.

4   The literacy educator had initiated a student support group in her literacy program. These comments came after she had been working with the group for a year.

Foundations of Reading

Introduction

If someone were to ask "What is your theory of reading?" how would you respond? If you have difficulty responding immediately, you are not alone. Research indicates that educators can usually discuss HOW they teach reading, but they are often unable to identify the theories on which their instruction is based (Bamberger, 1991). Most often, educators are not consciously aware of their belief systems, as they tend to devote all their attention to the act of teaching reading. Nevertheless, the approach that educators take to reading instruction is based upon a set of beliefs and implicit understandings that are formed and developed throughout their lives generally and their educational experiences in particular. Taken as a whole, these implicit and explicit beliefs and understandings form a theory of reading.

A questionnaire, such as the one illustrated in Figure 2.1 on the following page, is one way of identifying a personal theoretical orientation towards reading. As an illustrative exercise, read each statement and record your response. This brief exercise has the potential to indicate your personal theory of reading, and you will probably find that this theory falls under one of four broad classifications.

Before we continue, it should be noted that when it comes to reading theory, there is a paucity of research concerning how adults learn to read. Consequently, practitioners and academics have turned towards reading theories and models based primarily on the pedagogy of teaching reading to children. In the early 1970s, information processing theories in psychology were applied to reading, resulting in the development of two major reading theories: the text-based view (**bottom-up theory**) and the psycholinguistic view (**top-down theory**). By the late 1970s, educators' and psychologists' criticisms of these two theories resulted in the development of the **interactive theory** of the reading process. Starting in the

Figure 2.1 • Your Theory of Reading

	AGREE	DISAGREE	DEPENDS
1. The best way to identify an unfamiliar word is to predict or guess it.	☐	☐	☐
2. Literacy rates are lower among poor than rich people.	☐	☐	☐
3. Adults should strive for word perfect reading.	☐	☐	☐
4. A fluent reader uses a combination of prior knowledge and print cues to identify unfamiliar words.	☐	☐	☐
5. A fluent reader primarily uses prior knowledge to identify unfamiliar words.	☐	☐	☐
6. The meaning of a text is not fixed but socially constructed.	☐	☐	☐
7. Reading instruction should begin by teaching phonics.	☐	☐	☐
8. Readers combine their prior knowledge with text information to construct meaning.	☐	☐	☐
9. For beginning readers, learning letters and sounds is not a priority.	☐	☐	☐
10. Instruction should be based on a person's strengths and weaknesses, and his/her current level of ability to process print and text.	☐	☐	☐
11. Instruction should consider a person's social identity—his/her class, race, and gender.	☐	☐	☐
12. Reading is a hierarchy of skills, which should be taught sequentially.	☐	☐	☐

SOURCE: Some of these items are based on Campbell, P. & Brokop, F. (1998). *Supplemental training for practitioners in literacy education (STAPLE)*. Calgary, AB: Literacy Coordinators of Alberta.

1990s, there was a move away from information-processing theory that stress transmission of information processing towards a **social constructive theory** that views reading as a generative or meaning-making process. The sections that follow provide a more detailed look at these four theories. Before we proceed to this discussion, you might wish to begin classifying your theory of reading by reviewing your response to the statements in Figure 2.1.

- Agreement with Statements 3, 7, and 12 reflects a bottom-up theory of reading.
- Agreement with Statements 1, 5, and 9 reflects a top-down theory of reading.

- Agreement with Statements 4, 8, and 10 supports the interactive theory.
- Agreement with Statements 2, 6, and 11 supports a social constructive theory of reading.

Those statements to which you responded "Depends" also provide you with indicators of your reading theory. As you read the following descriptions, you may be able to discern which reading theory accommodates a "Depends" response as well as other such conditional responses.

Reading Theories

Bottom-up Theory

DEFINITION

According to this theory, also known as the "text-based" model, reading is primarily depicted as a perceptual process—the reader processes the information in the text by proceeding from part to whole. Consider the following instructional scenario in which instruction is based principally upon the bottom-up theory:

> Roxanne, a woman of colour, is in her early 20s. She enrolls in a community-based literacy program, hoping that upgrading will increase her employment opportunities. She is able to read and write her name, and recognize a few sight words such as "exit," "Pepsi," etc. During the first tutoring session, Roxanne and her tutor work through Lesson 1 in a reading workbook. Roxanne is introduced to the consonant "b," and performs some drill exercises for reinforcement. At the end of the lesson, Roxanne's tutor asks her to think of some words that begin with the letter "b." These words are printed on flash cards for future practice. The remaining lessons in the workbook focus on the consonant letters and sounds. Once Roxanne has mastered the consonants, she will begin a new workbook, designed to introduce her to the vowel sounds.

ASSUMPTIONS

As you can see from the sample lesson, the tutor is using an approach built on the belief that individuals learn to read by progressing through a linear, sequential series of skills (Gough, 1972). The assumption underlying this part-to-whole approach is that learning to read is easier if you start with small, separate pieces of information. Adults exposed to this approach master one skill at a time, beginning with the smallest unit of analysis (e.g., letters and sounds) and gradually moving to larger units such as words. Individuals focus on meaning only after they have developed their phonics knowledge to the point that processing print has reached a level of **automaticity**.

ASSESSMENT TOOLS

Assessment tools based on this theory do not provide the student with authentic reading experiences. Instead, the student is the passive recipient of reading tasks that consist of isolated, fragmented pieces of information. Assessment usually consists of a set of sub-tests, with each sub-test measuring a specific skill, such as word identification or word attack. Figure 2.2 contains the examiner's instructions for a word attack sub-test from the *Woodcock Reading Mastery Test* (1998). This sub-test, which reflects the bottom-up theory, assesses a student's word attack skills by having him/her read non-words in isolation.

Figure 2.2 • Word Attack Sample Item

>> **Say:** I want you to read some words that are not real words. I want you to tell me how they sound. Point to "tat." How does this word sound?

If the subject responds incorrectly, point to "tat" and say the word. Then point to "tat" again and say: Now try it again. How does this word sound?

SOURCE: Sample Word Attack Item A-B from the **Woodcock Reading Mastery Test-Revised (WMRT-R)** by Richard W. Woodcock © 1987 American Guidance Service, Inc., 4201 Woodland Road, Circle Pines, Minnesota USA 55014-1796. Reproduced with permission of publisher. All rights reserved. www.agsnet.com

PROBLEMS

This theory is based upon a deficit perspective, since the instructional focus is on the students' weaknesses—the reading skills they do not possess—rather than on their strengths, their knowledge, and reading skills they do possess. Since proponents of this theory believe that meaning resides in the text, the knowledge the reader brings to the text is not valued or taken into account as being important to the reader's construction of meaning or understanding of what has been read. The bottom-up theory is problematic, particularly among populations of adults with low literacy skills, because it ignores the role of their prior knowledge in constructing meaning. Instruction based on this theory can result in adults who think that reading consists of rote learning and does not take advantage of their major strength—an extensive reservoir of knowledge and experiences.

Top-down Theory

DEFINITION

According to this theory, reading is primarily a language-thinking or psycholinguistic process, with information processing proceeding from whole to part. Consider the following scenario in which instruction is based on the top-down theory:

> Chico, an older man who immigrated with his family from Mexico, is in his early 60s. He is enrolled in a family literacy program because he wants to read books to his grandchildren. His phonics knowledge is well-developed, but he does not use context cues to predict words. In addition, Chico does not usually correct his reading miscues if they do not make sense. His tutor brought a children's book to his first lesson. When Chico came across an unfamiliar word, he would try to sound it out. His tutor told Chico: "I do not want you to sound out words. Instead, read to the end of the sentence and try to 'guess' the word."

ASSUMPTIONS

The underlying theory in this example is based on the belief that readers use their knowledge about language and the world to form hypotheses about the meaning of texts (Smith, 1973). Then they sample only as much of the print as is necessary to confirm or disconfirm before revising the hypotheses (where necessary) and sampling more print. Readers use their knowledge of the syntactic and semantic systems in language to predict and confirm meaning, rather than relying wholly on their knowledge of phonics.

> ▶ The syntactic system refers the structure or word order of sentences. The semantic system refers to meaning.

ASSESSMENT TOOLS

Assessment tools based on top-down theory call for authentic measures such as portfolio assessment. A portfolio chronicles a student's growth as a reader and writer, although the emphasis in portfolio assessment is usually on writing. Measures of reading progress include reader response journals, dialogue journals, running records, and progress checklists. The *criteria* for evaluating these measures are somewhat vague, which means that instructors need to rely primarily on their professional judgment to infer instructional implications. Consequently, students may not receive specific and accurate feedback about their growth as readers.

PROBLEMS

The top-down theory, which is consistent with whole language approaches to instruction, can be problematic because it provides educators with few practical suggestions for instructional programs. Smith, a researcher who has written extensively about the psycholinguistic theory (1985, 1978, 1973, 1971), posed the following questions and responses:

What does a teacher do about a child who cannot read at all? How does the teacher get the child started in the literacy club? The answers to both questions are the same, since there is basically only one problem: how to facilitate reading for children when they can read very little or not at all. The answers can be summed up on one basic rule and guidelines for every aspect of reading instruction—make learning to read easy—which means making reading a meaningful, enjoyable, useful, and frequent experience for children. (Smith, 1985, p. 133)

It is apparent that Smith's one basic rule will not suffice for teachers who need practical advice. For some individuals immersion in a print-rich environment is not sufficient; they need explicit instruction in processing print and text. Smith (1983) has also pointed out that the "one difficult way to make learning to read easy" is to "respond to what the [learner] is trying to do" (p. 24). According to Smith, responsive instruction is difficult because it requires "insight, tolerance, sensitivity, and patience; it demands an understanding of the nature of reading, a rejection of formulae, less reliance on tests," and receptivity to the student (p. 24). In many ways responsive instruction reflects the concept of balance that forms the major thesis of this book.

Interactive Theory

DEFINITION

According to this theory, reading is primarily a cognitive process, and information processing proceeds from whole to part and part to whole (Rumelhart, 1977). The following instructional scenario portrays the key elements of interactive theory:

> Tirak, an Inuit man in his 30s, is enrolled in a workplace education program at a northern diamond mine. His word identification skills are well developed, but he has difficulty comprehending text. Tirak's program uses a combination of group and individual instruction. His first group lesson begins with a discussion on safety procedures, followed by silent reading of a safety manual. While the other members of the group engage in application and extension activities, the teacher provides Tirak with some individualized instruction. She begins by asking him, "What goes on in your head when you are reading something?" Tirak responds by saying "Nothing," which confirms the teacher's hypothesis that Tirak is not an overly "active" reader. He needs to learn specific strategies in order to understand and remember text information. The teacher uses the **"Think-aloud" strategy**, in which she models how she uses both her existing or prior knowledge along with the text information to comprehend the safety manual.

ASSUMPTIONS

The interactive theory of reading rests upon two assumptions about language, thinking, and learners (Lipson & Wixson, 1997). The first assumption is that reading is an active process of constructing meaning that occurs as the reader interacts with the text in a particular context or situation. Reader factors that affect meaning construction include the reader's prior knowledge of language, print, the reading process, and content, while text factors include text structure and structural features such as headings and illustrations. Contextual factors that influence reading include purpose (reading for information, enjoyment, or both), the setting (applying for a job, responding to a test, following a blueprint), and methods of instruction.

The second assumption is that readers use three language-cueing systems—graphophonic, syntactic, semantic—as they construct meaning. The graphophonic system refers to letters and sounds; when using this system, the reader analyzes the print cues in the text and makes predictions that are visually similar to the text. The syntactic system, commonly known as grammar, refers to the structure or word order of sentences; when using this system, the reader analyzes grammatical cues and makes predictions about unfamiliar words that "sound right." The semantic system refers to meaning; when using this system, the reader analyzes meaning cues and makes predictions about unfamiliar words that "make sense."

ASSESSMENT TOOLS

Informal reading inventories typify assessment tools based on this theory; they contain a set of graded reading passages and comprehension questions. During administration, the examiner can record the student's **miscues** during reading and the reader's **oral retelling** of the passage after reading. Through **miscue analysis**, the examiner can gain an understanding of which language-cueing systems the student uses to process print. By interpreting the student's oral retelling, the examiner can gain an understanding of how the student processes text in order to understand it.

PROBLEMS

Based on this theory, assessment and the instruction that follows is diagnostic, providing the student with an individualized program based upon his/her instructional reading level and current capabilities. You will want to note that this theory does not fully take into account the social and cultural factors that affect the readers' understanding of what they have read.

Social Constructivism

DEFINITION

According to this theory, reading is a process whereby meaning is socially constructed. The following example depicts a reading lesson presented from a social constructivist perspective.

Nilambri, who works at a literacy centre, facilitates a women's support group. The group is comprised of Mennonite and white Anglo-Saxon women. Together, the group develop the curriculum and choose topics for discussion. During the first lesson on stress, the group shares and analyzes their experiences. As part of the analysis, Nilambri facilitates a discussion on how their social identity contributes to the type of stress they have experienced. For example, the "wife's role" in the Mennonite family sometimes contributes to the stress experienced by Mennonite women. After reading and discussing several diverse selections on stress, the group identifies unfamiliar words that they found difficult to read. Nilambri presents a mini-lesson on how to use print and meaning cues to decode these words. The lesson ends with a brainstorming session on how to cope with the stress in their lives.

Proponents of social constructivism define reading as the active construction of meaning from cues in the text and from reader's background knowledge within a social context (Bainbridge & Malicky, 2000). This theory emphasizes the social construction of knowledge and meaning; what we think and what we know is viewed as a result of social experiences and interactions. Specifically, one's knowledge and ideas are related to cultural identity and shaped by ethnicity, primary language, gender, and social class.

The curriculum is built around the students' ownership of literacy rather than the simple attainment of skills. Ownership occurs when students value literacy: they have positive attitudes towards literacy and engage in literacy activities at home, at work, and in the community. Literature discussion groups, for example, promote students' ownership of literacy.

> ▶ Literature discussion groups provide an opportunity for students to converse about a book they have chosen to read. The instructor might initiate the group and may initially serve as a facilitator of the discussion. Eventually, the students take control of the discussion. The group consists of four to six students who meet for sessions of about 20 to 30 minutes.

When adults are responding to text in a group situation, the discussion can include how their different social identities (race, class, and gender) affect the way they understand the text. Such an approach provides opportunities for students to create their own understandings of literacy in the context of the various aspects of their lives (Au, 1998b).

A curriculum based on social constructivism uses multiple texts, which present various viewpoints about a topic. For example, students interested in reading about pregnancy and child birth are given information that represents the medical field, alternative medicine, and multicultural personal experiences. Students can examine the invisible messages and values within each piece of text to see if the author's values match their values.

ASSESSMENT TOOLS

Assessment tools based on this theory are culturally sensitive and provide opportunities for students to respond to what they read. The *Canadian Adult*

Reading Assessment (CARA) and the *Adult Diagnostic Reading Inventory (ADRI)* are examples of informal reading inventories based on the social constructivist theory of reading.[1] The passage topics were chosen by students from across Canada, in recognition of the diversity that exists among individuals in terms of race, class, and gender; and to reduce sources of cultural bias. The comprehension questions for fiction passages include a high percentage of **inference questions**, in order to acknowledge the important role that background knowledge plays in the individual's understanding of text. This contrasts with other informal reading inventories, in which the majority of the questions require direct recall of information in the text.

PROBLEMS

When this theory is translated into practice, problems may arise through misinterpretation. As an analogy, whole language has sometimes been misinterpreted, resulting in instruction that does not include the development of phonics knowledge. In a similar vein, some educators who believe in the social construction of knowledge may be reluctant to transmit knowledge; for example, they may not want to provide explicit phonics instruction. Yet the teaching of reading within a social constructivist framework acknowledges that explicit phonics instruction within a meaningful context may be necessary, depending upon the needs of the student(s) (Au, 1998b).

The Process of Learning to Read

READING INSTRUCTION is shaped by educators' knowledge of reading theories, and instruction is enhanced by an understanding of how children *and* adults learn to read. This section, which discusses the literacy development of children and adults, will provide insights into the compelling and controversial question, "How do people learn to read?" This discussion is followed by a set of principles, based on research from the field of emergent and adult literacy research, for teaching adult beginning readers.

The Literacy Development of Children

Emergent literacy is a term used to describe the early reading and writing development of young children. Emergent literacy knowledge, which encompasses the childrens' concepts, understanding, awareness, and attitudes towards written language, is shaped in response to childrens' initial literacy experiences in the home and the community (Purcell-Gates, 1998). The nature and level of their emergent literacy knowledge corresponds to the literacy culture in their home and community. Children raised in a print-rich literacy culture are constantly interacting with and observing significant others read and write. They have a greater opportunity to develop their emergent literacy knowledge than do children who are raised in an environment that offers limited literacy experiences. The point at which children become independent readers and writers marks the end of the emergent stage of literacy development.

Take a few minutes to reflect upon your early literacy experiences. Do you remember watching your parents engage in literacy activities? Were books lined up neatly on a bookshelf gathering dust or toppling over each other on coffee and bedside tables? Did your parents subscribe to a magazine and/or newspaper? Could your family afford to buy books or did you frequent the library? Did your family prefer to read, socialize, or play sports in their leisure time? Did your parents write letters, notes, and grocery lists? Did they encourage your attempts to print words and letters? Were you encouraged to recite your favourite nursery rhyme? Did your parents read to you before bedtime? Were you constantly asking how to spell certain words such as your name? Did you know the alphabet song? How did your early childhood experiences shape your attitude towards reading?

The question that continually sparks debate within the literacy field is "How do children learn to read?" Although this question remains contentious, some generalizations appear to be substantially supported. In the first place, it is now generally accepted that during the emergent stage of literacy development, children are developing their *awareness* of the nature of written language and its relationship to spoken language. This awareness serves as the conceptual foundation for their growth as readers and writers.

Children's awareness of the relationship between written language and speech is heightened through their interactions with print. During their pre-school years, children learn about the *functions of written language* (why people read and write) through being read to and through observing family members using reading and writing for a variety of purposes. Just think of the daily literacy activities that occur in many homes. Children see their parents prepare meals by following a recipe, or they see a family member read instructions to build a barbeque or a model airplane. They see their mother laugh when she reads a cartoon in the newspaper or frown when she reads something tragic. Through these observations, children learn that written language contains meaning—it can provide information and pleasure.

When children are read to, the notion that books provide pleasure is reinforced. When they realize that books tell stories, children begin to create their own stories when they open up a book and attempt to "read" it. Children develop an awareness of the *conventions of written language* when they cuddle up with their parents and listen to stories. By watching their parents read, children begin to understand that one reads from left to right and from the top of the page to the bottom. Through repeated exposure to written language, they begin to see that sentences start with a capital letter and end with a period. As well, children may begin to form a concept for terms such as "letter" and "word." They are learning the "instructional code," the specialized language of instruction that they will encounter from their teacher when they enter a formal educational setting.

Just like their favourite teddy, children often have a favourite book. By reading the same book over and over again, children begin to memorize the story. Through repeated readings, children begin to engage in eye-voice matching, which means they match the words on the page with the words stored in their memory. They can actually point to a word in a story book and say it. In time, children begin to understand that the letters in written words stand for sounds in spoken words. The development of *phonemic awareness* is perhaps the most important early understanding that readers construct about print (Bainbridge & Malicky, 2000).

If children are raised in homes where they are read to and where they observe others engaged in reading and writing practices, they develop awareness about the relationship between written language and speech. In fact, studies (Purcell-Gates, 1996; Purcell-Gates & Dahl, 1991) have documented that "simply counting the number of times that someone in the home reads or writes anything will predict the degree to which young children in that home know that print is meaningful and that it functions purposively in people's lives" (Purcell-Gates, 2000, p. 62). According to research, the degree to which children understand the functions of written language at the beginning of kindergarten will predict their degree of success at reading and writing at the end of first grade and their growth as readers and writers (Purcell-Gates & Dahl, 1991). If a child is not raised in a literate environment, he/she will be at a considerable disadvantage when beginning formal literacy instruction, and may experience difficulty in learning to read and write.

The Literacy Development of Adults

Traditionally, research in the field of emergent literacy has focused its lens on young children rather than adults. In a study that examined the characteristics of research on reading between 1969 and 1998, only 3 percent of the studies involved adults as research participants (Guzzetti, Anders & Neuman, 1999). According to McGee and Purcell-Gates (1997), more research is needed on how adults learn to read. They write:

> ... I do not believe we can map what we conceptualize now as emergent literacy very well onto what adults go through. It's an interesting area for study, though, and increasingly relevant as the field looks more and more into adult learning/literacy. (p. 311)

Because there are obvious differences between adults and children, we cannot assume that both groups learn to read in the same way. For instance, in comparison to children, adults possess a high degree of knowledge based on past experiences and an extensive vocabulary. In their day-to-day lives, adults are constantly solving problems, honing their abilities to analyze and synthesize information. Adults are continually making inferences during their social interactions with others. The question that remains to be answered is this: How do adults' strengths, in terms of their cognitive development and life experiences, affect the learning to read process?

Unfortunately, many adults who are learning to read often face more barriers than children. One of the major barriers is the way that adults view themselves and their chances of becoming literate. Many times, adults have hesitantly asked me: "Do you think I can learn to read?" or "Will my reading get better?" Imagine the courage required to even ask these questions. Because of their early experiences and encounters with literacy, adults often have a negative view of themselves as readers, underestimating their ability to read and write (Malicky, Katz, Norton & Norman, 1997). Their fear of reading reduces their willingness to take risks and "guess" at words, both of which are essential attributes of the beginning reader. In addition, material constraints such as time,

> ▶ **Because there are obvious differences between adults and children, we cannot assume that both groups learn to read in the same way.**

childcare, money, and transportation present barriers for adults who are learning to read. Children, for instance, usually have all the time in the world, whereas adults are inevitably constrained by the responsibilities of work, community, and family. Often short on time, adults generally approach learning to read and reading in general as a serious endeavour, unlike children, who can approach reading much more playfully.

In a recent study, Dr. Grace Malicky and I examined the reading strategies used by adults in the early stages of literacy development (2002). This study did not ask "How do adults learn to read?" Rather, we asked, "What are the word identification and comprehension strategies of beginning readers?" By examining the strategies used by adult beginning readers, we were able to draw implications about effective instruction.

An important finding of this research is that beginning readers relied primarily upon either meaning-based strategies or an integrated use of meaning- and print-based strategies as they read. They focused more heavily on using what they brought with them to the learning context and their background knowledge than on what was new: the print itself.

The following examples illustrate a beginning adult reader's miscues. In Example 1, the reader is relying primarily on background knowledge to predict the text word, while in Example 2, the reader is using a combination of background knowledge and print to predict the text words:

Example 1

Text: Wet mitts hung near the stove.

Student: Wet mitts hung near the fire.

See how the reader used his/her prior knowledge to predict the word "fire." Note how "fire" contains only one of the letters in the text word "stove." This suggests that the reader used primarily meaning-based strategies to identify the word.

Example 2

Text: Run up and down the stairs.

Student: Run up and down the street.

In this case, the reader analyzed some of the print information (the letters "s," "t," and "r"), and then used his/her prior knowledge to predict a word that made sense in the context of the sentence. This suggests an integrated use of meaning and print-based strategies.

SOME IMPLICATIONS FOR INSTRUCTION

The adults' reliance on *meaning cues* or a combination of *meaning and print cues* suggests that programs emphasizing and reinforcing use of background knowledge to identify words and construct meaning *are* appropriate for beginning readers. The advantage of literacy programs that emphasize use of knowledge-based information is that instruction begins with what adults bring to programs—what they already know—rather than with what they do not know. This does not mean that strategies for processing print should be neglected. However, one of the major goals of an effective literacy program is to help readers integrate their reading strategies rather than relying excessively on any one strategy.

The disadvantage of instructional programs that emphasize use of knowledge-based information is that there can be a mismatch between the adults' expectations and the curriculum. Adults who were exposed to phonics instruction during primary school may expect a similar form of instruction from their tutor or classroom teachers. Consequently, they may think that producing a **language experience story** does not reflect "real" reading. If this is the case, it may be necessary from the outset for educators and students to discuss and share their concepts of reading and literacy instruction. If this discussion does not take place, students may become frustrated with the instruction they are receiving because it does not match their expectations.

Principles for Teaching Adult Beginning Readers

THE FOLLOWING PRINCIPLES are based on research from the field of emergent and adult literacy research.

> Instruction is linked to assessment.

Some literacy instructors question the point of assessing an adult who *can't* read. Yet, even adults who view themselves as *non-readers* possess literacy knowledge and skills that are critical in planning a responsive instructional program. Insightful, diagnostic assessment provides opportunities for students to demonstrate what they can do, rather than what they cannot do. Once they are determined, the students' abilities—what they are able to do—form the foundation of their instructional program. As they plan and develop effective instructional programs for students, educators also use diagnostic measures to gather information about the student's goals, interests, and conceptual understanding of reading.

> Instruction includes discussion about the students' conceptual understanding of reading.

Students may have restricted notions about what it means to be a reader and about how one learns to read. Their misconceptions about reading might hinder their ability to learn, so it is important for educators and students to share views and discuss differences of opinion. By providing opportunities for group discussion, students will gain a deeper and clearer understanding of what it means to be a reader.

An excellent starting point is the question "Why do people read?" Beginning readers may approach each piece of text in the same way, whether they are attempting to read a discount coupon or a report card. Through discussion, students learn that people approach text in different ways, depending on their purpose for reading it.

Responses to the question "What does it mean to be a good reader?" can provide valuable information about why students prefer certain strategies over others. For instance, if adults were exposed to phonics instruction during their primary education, they may believe that good readers sound out every letter, and "guessing" unfamiliar words is a form of "cheating." If this is the case, instructors can broaden and deepen students' concept of reading by discussing how good readers use their background knowledge to decode and interpret a piece of text. By asking questions such as "What do you do when you come across a word you don't know?" and "What do you do if you don't understand something you have read?" instructors gain insight into the students' awareness and knowledge of reading strategies.

> Instruction builds upon the students' expectations and intentions.

Students usually come to the program with expectations about how they will be taught to read and the time it will take to them to become fluent readers. Students need opportunities to share their expectations so that educators and students can come to a common understanding. If discussion does not occur, students may experience frustration and anger because their expectations are not being met. If a student lacks confidence and views the instructor as the "expert," she/he may leave the program rather than express dissatisfaction. Without fully understanding the situation, the instructor may label a student as unmotivated. Or students may hope to become literate within a short time frame, and if this does not occur, they will become disheartened.

> Reading instruction is integrated and balanced.

Rather than focusing primarily on word identification skills as a prerequisite, educators who use a balanced approach focus on the development of reading strategies for both comprehension *and* word identification throughout the students' instructional program.

> Students are expected to take responsibility and ownership of their learning, and educators to provide opportunities for them to do so.

Some students restrict their reading to the instruction that occurs within the four walls of the classroom. Once the students leave for the day, their engagement in literacy activities may be limited. These students need to understand the importance of transferring and applying their literacy skills into the home and community. Students develop these understandings primarily when they feel responsible for each stage and aspect of their learning, from onset to completion. In situations where the instructor retains most of the control, students may become so dependent on the instructor that they adopt a passive role in their learning. Ownership comes when students assume responsibility for clarifying their intentions, setting learning goals and timeframes for completion, evaluating and reflecting on progress, and assessing what they have learned in terms of relevance and utility.

> The instructional program responds to the needs of each individual student.

A recent study has shown that beginning adult readers use different reading strategies to decode unfamiliar words (Campbell & Malicky, 2002). There are differences in the degree to which they rely on print-based and knowledge-based information and on their ability to integrate these two sources of information. Consequently, the notion of "one program for all" will not meet the needs of individual students, so group instruction should be supplemented by individualized instruction.

Students who rely too heavily on print cues need instruction that places a heavier focus on meaning. These students will benefit from instruction in the **Cloze procedure**. If students rely too heavily on their background or personal knowledge, the meanings they construct will bear little resemblance to that intended by the author. These students need instruction that places a heavier focus on strategies for processing print *and* text information. They will benefit from instruction in the **ReQuest procedure** or the **Herringbone technique**.

> Instruction emphasizes the student's knowledge.

Research has shown that adult beginning readers primarily use either meaning-based strategies or a combination of meaning- and print-based strategies to decode unfamiliar words. (Campbell & Malicky, 2002). Several instructional techniques and materials serve to elicit and utilize a student's background knowledge (Campbell & Brokop, 1998). When students read language experience stories or locally produced reading material that reflects their experiences, they are more likely to use their background knowledge to predict unfamiliar words. Rather than sounding out new words, students can be asked to predict words that make sense. Comprehension activities such as **Directed Reading Thinking Activity (DRTA)** (Stauffer, 1975) and **K-W-L** (Ogle, 1986) encourage students to activate their background knowledge and relate it to text information.[2]

Many beginning readers tend to make numerous miscues as they attempt to read. Rather than drawing attention to these miscues, instructors should provide encouragement when meaningful miscues are made. Comments such as "That word makes sense" will promote the use of meaning to identify words. Placing emphasis on producing meaning rather than on word-perfect reading encourages students to take risks.

> When needed, phonics instruction is integrated into lessons.

When students need phonics instruction, it is embedded in meaningful contexts and introduced at appropriate times throughout the reading lesson. Rather than being taught phonics in a sequential fashion, phonics skills are introduced on an as-needed basis. Also, rather than being taught phonics skills in isolation, they are taught in context. If, for example, the student is unable to use meaning to decode a word such as "movie" in his/her language experience story, the educator teaches a phonics lesson on the letter "m." By teaching in this fashion, the educator is seizing "teachable moments."

> Reading material is relevant and authentic.

For many adult non-readers, "reading materials" may be associated with a type of basal text which focuses more on controlled vocabulary and language structures than on meaningful content. Reading material that is interesting and relevant to students' lives, and within the range of their current reading ability or level, helps them to realize that written language is generally meaningful. Since it is often difficult to find this type of text, especially for beginning adult readers, language experience stories can be used. Language experience stories present authentic, connected text that help students to realize the ways that semantic, syntactic, and graphophonic cues can be combined to help them read fluently. As students grow as readers, the instructor's and students' choices of commercial text continue to be guided by authenticity and their compatibility with the readers' current reading ability level.

> Opportunities are provided for interactive learning.

Studies have shown that students value a sense of community in their literacy programs. Their strong desire for community points to the need to challenge the "each one teach one" concept that still pervades literacy instruction throughout North America. The primary way in which students can begin to see that personal problems are social issues is through talking to each other. These conversations can be the springboard for dialogue, for a contextualized literacy education that recognizes the collective, social purpose of education, rather than a decontextualized, depoliticized functional education that stresses the skill needs of the individual learner.

C H A P T E R S U M M A R Y

Although educators may not be able to specifically define or explain the theory on which their instructional programs are based, their practice is based on a theory of reading. This chapter has reviewed four major reading theories: top-down, bottom-up, interactive, and social constructivism. For each of these theories, illustrative examples of assessment and curriculum development were presented and discussed. The two theories most closely aligned with a balanced approach to teaching reading are the interactive and the social constructive theories as these theories stress the importance of print (text cues) *and* meaning.

You were invited to make a tentative identification of your theory and test it against the discussion of the reading process and how this process applies to the literacy development of both children and adults. At this time there is a need for more research into how adults learn to read, as most adult reading programs are currently based on the findings of research into children's literacy development. Notwithstanding the lack of research, it is readily apparent that adults bring a different and more complex set of understandings to learning to read than do children. Some of these factors, such as maturity and experience, directly support programming efforts, while others, such as restricted notions of how reading is learned, may need to be discussed in order for a program to be effective.

A critical set of *Principles for Teaching Adult Beginning Readers* was presented. These principles form the central themes and aspects of balance that are discussed in the chapters that follow:

- Instruction is integrated and balanced.
- Instruction is linked to assessment.
- Students are expected to take responsibility and ownership of their learning, and educators to provide opportunities for them to do so.
- The instructional program responds to the needs of each individual student.
- Instruction includes discussion about the students' conceptual understanding of reading.
- Instruction builds upon the students' expectations and intentions.
- When needed, phonics instruction is integrated into lessons.
- Reading material is relevant and authentic.
- Opportunities are provided for interactive learning. ❧

References

Au, K.H. (1998a). Social constructivism and the school literacy learning of students of diverse backgrounds. *Journal of Literacy Research*, *30* (2), 297-319.

Au, K.H. (1998b). Constructivist approaches, phonics, and the literacy learning of students of diverse backgrounds. In T. Shanahan & F.V. Rodriguez-Brown (Eds.), *National reading conference yearbook 47*. Chicago: National Reading Conference.

Bainbridge, J. & Malicky, G. (2000). *Constructing meaning: Balancing elementary language arts* (2nd ed.). Toronto, ON: Harcourt Canada.

Bamberger, J. (1991). The laboratory for making things: Developing multiple representations of knowledge. In D. A. Schön (Ed.), *The reflective turn: Case studies in and on educational practice*. New York: Teachers College Press.

Campbell, P. & Brokop, F. (1998). *Supplemental training for practitioners in literacy education (STAPLE)*. Calgary, AB: Literacy Coordinators of Alberta. Distributed by Grass Roots Press.

Campbell, P. & Brokop, F. (2000). *Canadian adult reading assessment*. Edmonton, AB: Grass Roots Press.

Campbell, P. & Brokop, F. (2001). *Adult diagnostic reading inventory*. Edmonton, AB: Grass Roots Press.

Campbell, P. & Malicky. G. (2002). The reading strategies of adult basic education students. *Adult Basic Education*, *12*(1), 3-19.

Gough, P.B. (1972). One second of reading. In H. Singer & R. Ruddell (Eds.), *Theoretical models and processes of reading*. Newark, DE: International Reading Association.

Guzzetti, B., Anders, P.L., & Neuman, S. (1999). Thirty years of JRB/JLR: A retrospective of reading/literacy research. *Journal of Literacy Research*, *31*(1), 67-92.

Lipson, M.Y. & Wixson, K.K. (1997). *Assessment and instruction of reading and writing disability: An interactive approach*. New York: Longman.

Malicky, G.V., Katz, C.H., Norton, M. & Norman, C.A. (1997). Literacy learning in a community-based program. *Adult Basic Education*, *7* (2), 84-103.

McGee, L.M. & Purcell-Gates, V. (1997). "So what's going on in research on emergent literacy?" *Reading Research Quarterly*, *32*, 310-318.

Ogle, D.M. (1986). K-W-L: A teaching model that develops active reading of expository text. *Reading Teacher*, *39*(6), 564-570.

Purcell-Gates, V. (1996). Stories, coupons and the TV guide: Relationships between home literacy experiences and emergent literacy knowledge. *Reading Research Quarterly*, *31*(4), 406-428.

Purcell-Gates, V. (1998). Growing successful readers: Homes, communities, and schools. In J. Osborn and F. Lehr (Eds.), *Literacy for all: Issues in teaching and learning* (pp. 51-72). New York: The Guilford Press.

Purcell-Gates, V. (2000). *Affecting change in literacy practices of adult learners: Impact of two dimensions of instruction* (NCSALL Report #17). Cambridge, MA: Harvard Graduate School of Education, The National Center for the Study of Adult Learning and Literacy.

Purcell-Gates, V. & Dahl, K. (1991). Low-SES children's success and failure at early literacy learning in skills-based classrooms. *JRB: A Journal of Literacy, 23*, 1-34.

Rumelhart, D.E. (1977). *Introduction to human information processing theory.* New York: John Wiley & Sons.

Smith, F. (1971). *Understanding reading: A psycholinguistic analysis of reading and learning to read.* Toronto, ON: Holt, Rinehart and Winston, Inc.

Smith, F. (1973). *Psycholinguistics and reading.* Toronto, ON: Holt, Rinehart, and Winston, Inc.

Smith, F. (1978). *Reading.* Port Chester, NY: Cambridge University Press.

Smith, F. (1983). *Essays into literacy: Selected papers and some afterthoughts.* Exeter, NH: Heinemann.

Smith, F. (1985). *Reading without nonsense.* New York: Teacher's College Press.

Stauffer, R.G. (1975). *Directing the reading-thinking process.* New York: Harper & Row.

Woodcock, R.W. (1987). *The Woodcock reading mastery tests – revised.* Circle Pines, MN: American Guidance Service.

Notes

1   The *Adult Diagnostic Reading Inventory* is the American version of the *Canadian Adult Reading Assessment.*

2   See Chapter Five for more information on DRTA and K-W-L.

CHAPTER THREE

Assessment

Introduction

When it comes to assessment, the two questions that educators most often ask are "What is the best way to assess reading?" and "What is the most appropriate tool to use in our program?" The quick answer to both questions is, "It depends," since many factors dictate what assessment tool is chosen. The educators' decisions are influenced by four key factors:

- The purpose for using the assessment.
- The educators' experience with and knowledge of reading and assessment.
- The educational policies and contexts surrounding the assessment.
- Situational constraints such as available materials, time, and funding.

Each of these factors will influence to some degree the assessment decisions that the educator makes; however, depending upon the situation, one factor may exert a more powerful influence than do the others. Consider three common scenarios. First, an instructor might want to engage in an in-depth assessment to determine a student's instructional needs, but due to time constraints, is able to administer only group assessments that provide placement information. Second, an educator with experience in administering standardized assessments might be hesitant about adopting a new type of assessment tool that requires a level of interpretive skills beyond his or her current level of expertise. Third, a literacy coordinator might believe in the value of authentic assessment for the purposes of placement and diagnosis, but government policy dictates the use of competency-based assessment tools for the purpose of accountability.

The term "assessment" evokes strong emotional responses among stakeholders in adult literacy. Students might grimace and groan as they recall experiences from their youth, educators might raise a flurry of ethical and pragmatic questions, while funders and administrators might discuss the need for accountability. Since each stakeholder has a vested interest in assessment and its uses, it is important to understand that assessment comes in many forms and variations and serves a variety of purposes.

It is against this backdrop that this chapter explores two questions: "What is the best way to assess reading?" and "What is the most appropriate tool to use in our program?" It begins with an overview of three types of assessment tools: standardized tests, competency-based assessment, and authentic assessment. Each form of assessment is discussed under the following headings: description, background, links to instruction, and critique. Since the issue of using assessment to diagnose learning disabilities is contentious among some literacy educators, the chapter concludes by exploring the notion of labelling students and the consequences of such labelling.

Types of Assessment for Adult Learners

COMMUNITY COLLEGES, school boards, and community-based literacy programs use a variety of reading assessments that are distinguished by the reading theories on which they are based, the reading skills and abilities they purport to measure and provide, and the manner in which they inform instruction. In adult literacy programs, assessment tools that measure and document reading performance can be classified into three groups: standardized tests, competency-based assessment, and authentic assessment.

- Standardized tests produce an individual "score" that can be compared, with both the individual's previous scores and the scores of others who have taken the test.
- Competency-based assessment compares the individual's performance against a set of predefined, specified skills or competency outcomes. These competencies are generally tied to curricular content.
- Authentic assessment provides information about an individual's reading performance, without comparing that individual's performance to others.

Standardized Tests

DESCRIPTION

The term "standardized" means that the tests are always administered and scored the same way. The term "norm-referenced" means that the tests compare a student's performance with the performance of a **norm** group. Adult literacy educators administer a variety of standardized, norm-referenced tests such as the *Tests of Adult Basic Education, Forms 7 and 8* (TABE 7 & 8), the *Canadian Adult Achievement Test* (CAAT), the *Nelson-Denny Reading Test*, the *Standard Diagnostic Reading Test*, the *Gates-MacGinitie Reading Tests*, and the *Woodcock Reading Mastery Test–Revised*. Only two of these tests—the CAAT and the TABE—were designed specifically for the adult population.

The Canadian Adult Achievement Test

The CAAT is the only test normed on Canadians *and* on an adult population. Four levels of CAAT have been developed, with each level corresponding to years of formal education. Level A, for instance, is for adults who have completed one to four years of formal education (the primary grades). The CAAT consists of a battery of five sub-tests: vocabulary, reading comprehension, spelling, number operations, and problem solving. The reading comprehension sub-test in Level A contains 42 comprehension questions. The text or stimulus material includes signs, reading passages presented in a modified **cloze** format, and short reading passages, all followed by multiple-choice questions. Levels B and C each consist of 9 passages that include material of a functional nature (signs, advertisements, letters, etc) and material of an educational nature. Each passage is followed by a series of 4 to 7 factual and inferential multiple-choice questions. (Figure 3.1 illustrates a sample reading comprehension activity from the reading comprehension sub-test of the CAAT Level B.) Level D uses three types of text—functional, fiction, and non-fiction—to assess literal, inferential, and critical comprehension. Although the CAAT is intended for adults, the norming sample tended to involve primarily young adults. The *Norms Booklet* shows that 32 percent of the norming sample were in the 18-to-22 year age range and an additional 45 percent were in the 25-to-34 year age range.

Figure 3.1 • Reading Comprehension Activity

Rose Ann Robbins, M.D.
Is pleased to announce
the opening of her practice of
FAMILY MEDICINE
1505 Grand Ave., Room 768
Phone: 875-2333

A This ad tells about the opening of a –

a family.
b hospital.
c medical practice.
d school.

B If you went there, you would be treated by a –

e doctor
f dentist.
g veterinarian.
h lawyer.

SOURCE: Harcourt Brace & Company and The Psychological Association. (1988). *Canadian adult achievement test*. Level B Test Booklet. Toronto, ON: Author. Permission granted to reprint.

The Tests of Adult Basic Education

The TABE 9 and 10[1] are designed to measure achievement in four basic areas: reading, language, mathematics, and spelling. Five levels of TABE have been developed, with each level corresponding to target grade ranges. Level L corresponds to Grade 0 – 1.9, while Level A corresponds to Grades 9 to 12.9. The reading sub-test in Level L has 50 items that screen students for visual/reversal problems, recognition of letters, and auditory and comprehension skills. The reading sub-test for each of the remaining 4 levels contains 50 questions that measure the student's ability to construct meaning from a variety of life skills and prose selections. Although these tests are intended for adults, the technical report does not provide any information on the age of the norming sample. The sample was drawn from students in four reference groups: adult basic education, vocational/technical, adult/juvenile offender and college programs. With this information, it may be assumed that the norming sample, with the exception of the juvenile offenders, was over the age of eighteen years.

BACKGROUND

> Changes in assessment technology over the last two centuries—from oral to written, from qualitative to quantitative, from short answer to multiple choice—were all geared toward increasing efficiency and making the assessment system more manageable, standardized, easily administered, objective, reliable, comparable, and inexpensive, particularly as the numbers of examinees increased. (Madaus & O'Dwyer, 1999, p. 689)

At the turn of the 20th century, the first standardized tests based on the concept of norm-referenced scoring were introduced into North American public school systems (Anastasi, 1988; Madaus & O'Dwyer, 1999). These tests were valued for several reasons:

- Scores could be used to compare student performance across schools and school districts.
- Administration and scoring were cost-efficient.
- The tests utilized psychometric measures of **reliability** and **validity**, enabling teachers to make inferences and generalizations from test scores.

Today, adult literacy educators primarily use standardized test scores to place students in appropriate programs.

LINKING STANDARDIZED TESTING TO INSTRUCTION

Standardized tests provide little information about the student's reading strategies and what needs to be taught in order to foster literacy development. Standardized tests tend to reflect a simplistic, skills-based notion of the reading process; reading is segmented into skill areas such as vocabulary, comprehension, and word identification. These skill areas are usually measured through multiple-choice questions or tasks with single answers. If the educator uses the test results to describe a student's literacy development, the description is succinct, general, and standardized, rather than extensive, specific, and personalized (Johnston, 1998). For instance, if an educator administered the *Canadian Adult Achievement Test* (CAAT), the description or interpretation might read as follows: "Moira's total test score was Grade 4.5 in reading." In this case, the link between assessment and instruction is very tenuous. If educators looked to the content or actual test items as concrete indications of what the student needs to learn in order to become a fluent reader, the result would be decontextualized, skills-based instruction with a relatively narrow focus. For instance, students might be assigned to read a passage and answer a set of multiple-choice comprehension questions. Rather than learning how to construct meaning from text, they would continue to practice skills that are needed only for responding to multiple-choice questions. In addition, assessing comprehension through multiple-choice questions reinforces the notion that there is only one right answer for every question. Students may conclude that if there is only one right answer, everyone must interpret text in the same way. When this notion is linked to instruction, students become passive learners concerned with providing the "right" answer, rather than learners integrating their knowledge with text to construct meaning and make inferences.

> ▶ Standardized tests provide little information about the student's reading strategies and what needs to be taught in order to foster literacy development. Standardized tests tend to reflect a simplistic, skills-based notion of the reading process; reading is segmented into skill areas such as vocabulary, comprehension, and word identification.

CRITIQUE

Although standardized tests provide information that may be used to place a student in an adult basic education class, they do not take into consideration the fact that students' performances on the test are affected by factors such as testing conditions, their skill in and experience with answering multiple-choice questions, physical condition, their ability to interpret instructions, and their emotional state of mind. This means that an adult might achieve a grade score of 4.5 on a "good day" and 3.8 on an "off day" (Bainbridge & Malicky, 2000). Because of this variation and the factors discussed above, placement should be based on a combination of interview information, grade scores, common sense, and intuition.

Due to the diversity of students attending adult basic education classes, institutions want to use assessment tools that are "fair" and without "bias." Consequently, the popularity of standardized tests rests on claims for their objectivity. This begs the question, If objectivity is valued, what is devalued? Hansen (1998) argues that standardized "tests are not designed to show the details of rich, individual differences; they devalue diversity. Instead, everyone is simply above or below a standard" (p. 113). Many educators question whether the claim that standardized tests are objective has any validity at all. They question the extent to which race, class, and gender **biases** are built into the construction, and even the administration and scoring practices of these tests.

Johnston (1998) writes that "because of the cultural nature of literacy, it is not possible to create an unbiased literacy test; tests always privilege particular forms of language and experience" (p. 98). For example, consider the proper nouns used in the *Canadian Adult Achievement Test* – Level A: Robert, George, Joan, Sally, Ted, Bill, and Pat. There is no doubt that these names reflect the Anglo-Saxon population. In an unbiased or bias-free test, names that represented a variety of cultures such as Yin, Chandra, Ali, Enooya, and Corizon would be used. In Level D, one of the reading selections is a poem followed by a question that requires understanding of the terms "flashback," "metaphor," "imagery," and "irony." This question privileges adults who have attended public school and learned the language used to study literature.

> ▶ Bias occurs in testing when items systematically measure differently for different ethnic, gender, or age groups. Test developers reduce bias by analyzing item data separately for each group, then identifying and discarding items that appear to be biased.

When considering objectivity further, one must ask such questions as: Who constructs these tests? Who decides the wording and content of the items? and Who decides what counts as correct answers? Perhaps tests are biased in favor of students whose culture and upbringing most closely resemble that of the test makers—typically, white middle-class males and females who live in urban areas. When any test reflects narrowly defined cultural values, students with diverse backgrounds will not be fairly assessed.

Standardized tests are valued by some educators because they may be able to draw inferences about students' reading knowledge and/or skills based on their test results. Yet, should an educator rely on inferences about achievement drawn from a single performance that might or might not represent what the individual student knows or can do? Moreover, should the educator make inferences when the test's validity is questionable? For example, is a test such as the *Woodcock Reading Mastery Tests*, in which the total reading score reflects primarily performance on word identification sub-tests and only one comprehension sub-test, a valid measure of reading?

Finally, standardized tests are usually administered in a group setting, which means that there is little opportunity for the student and the assessor to develop rapport; rather, relationship between the student and assessor is impersonal and distant. For adults returning to school with limited self-confidence in their academic abilities, such a situation may create an intimidating, high-anxiety environment.

In conclusion, although educators and administrators can usually cite the shortcomings of standardized tests, they may be obliged to use these tests due to educational policies and constraints such as time and funding. In addition, educators who do not feel confident or competent to administer and interpret a diagnostic reading assessment might choose to administer a standardized assessment. Given the current movement towards higher levels of program accountability, the use of these tests will likely increase. With these caveats in mind, the guiding principle for educators in selecting a standardized test remains its appropriateness for the student population being assessed. In cases where educators are required to use standardized testing, the questions in Figure 3.2 can serve as a useful framework for evaluating its appropriateness. The answers to Questions 2, 3, 4 and 9 can usually be found in the examiner's manual.

Figure 3.2 • Criteria for Evaluating Standardized Tests

1. Is the test appropriate for the intended purpose(s)?

2. Does the norming sample represent the student population?

3. Is the alternate-form reliability measure high enough to warrant using the test for entrance and exit assessments?

4. What research was conducted to determine desired test content/and or evaluate content?

5. How similar is the test's content to the content you are interested in testing and/or teaching?

6. Will test administrators understand precisely what is expected of them?

7. How are test results reported?

8. What materials and resources are available to aid in interpreting test results?

9. Were the test items analyzed statistically for possible bias? What method(s) was used?

10. What extra difficulties does the test present for non-native speakers of English?

SOURCES: American Educational Research Association, American Psychological Association & National Council on Measurement in Education. (1999). *Standards for educational and psychological testing.* Washington, DC: American Educational Research Association

Rudner, L.M. (1994). *Questions to ask when evaluating tests.* Washington, DC: ERIC Clearinghouse on Assessment and Evaluation. (ERIC Document Reproduction Service No. ED385607)

Competency-based Assessment

DESCRIPTION

Competency-based assessment takes the reader, the task, the text, and the context into account. This type of assessment is intended to be used to assess the students' specific reading skills in order to determine what they know and can do in *specified contexts*, and to map their performance against descriptive criteria within a competencies **matrix** or rubric.

Students perform demonstration activities in which they demonstrate the skills they have learned by performing real-life activities. Demonstrations show that students can integrate and apply the skills or competencies they have learned in a specific activity that is related to their goals. Practitioners can either build their own demonstration activity or use published demonstrations such as those found in the assessment tool, *Common Assessment of Basic Skills (CABS).*

Figure 3.3 is a demonstration task from *CABS* that can be used to assess Level 1 reading skills. By asking the student to read the bulletin board notice, the practitioner can gain insight into whether the student:

- Uses knowledge of alphabet and basic phonics to decode common words.
- Uses context cues and personal experience to gather meaning from the text.
- Reads symbols and common sight words from everyday life.

Figure 3.3 • Demonstration Task for Level 1 Reading Skills

Bulletin Board Notice

Lost

Woman's white hand bag
In City Park
Last Friday, April 20th
Contains pills and make-up
Please call Mary at 421-7589

REWARD

SOURCE: Fox Lee, J. & Strohmaier, R. (2000). *Common assessment of basic skills (CABS): Initial assessment in 5 levels* (3rd ed.). Kingston, ON: Literacy Link Eastern Ontario. Permission granted to reprint.

BACKGROUND

During the 1990s, and particularly after the publication of the *International Adult Literacy Survey* (1996), federal, provincial, and territorial governments began to emphasize the linkages between literacy training and sustainable employment. These links were evident in the various government-issued mission statements that contain guiding principles and objectives for their adult literacy and basic skills programs, as well as in the funding of workplace, vocational, and training programs. The focus of the Literacy and Basic Skills Program (LBS) in Ontario is a case in point:

> The LBS Program delivery services focus on people who are unemployed, with a special emphasis on social assistance recipients. The program is, however, also open to employed Ontarians who need to improve their literacy skills in order to maintain or upgrade their work skills. (Ministry of Education and Training, 1998, p. 7)

In order for the public purse to remain open, the federal and provincial governments realized that accountability frameworks needed to be established to ensure that literacy services were cost-effective and efficient, and produced measurable results. This led to the development of standards-based systems that encompassed competency-based assessment, competency-based education, and accreditation. According to Kerka (1995), "the competency standards movement in Britain, Australia, New Zealand, and the United States (are also) closely tied to political initiatives for global competitiveness and accountability" (p. 2). The assumption underlying accountability frameworks is that if there are clear expectations, teachers will know what they are supposed to teach, students will see how hard they must work to make the grade, and taxpayers will know whether the population is becoming more literate.

By the year 2000, every Canadian province and territory was working towards the development and implementation of an accountability framework. Each government was positioned at a different point along the accountability continuum. At one end of the continuum were governments, like Ontario's, that developed a multi-year reform addressing accountability through a four-phase approach: learning outcomes, common assessment, articulation, and recognition. At the other end of the continuum were governments, such as those in Alberta and Saskatchewan, that funded the development of program standards but did not mandate them. The primary accountability measures for these two provinces were (1) whether the programs met their own objectives and (2) output measures such as the number of learners and volunteer tutors who participated in the program.

With the introduction of accountability frameworks, assessment became a "hot" topic. Governments and literacy providers promoted the concept of "common assessment" in order to enhance articulation and portability among delivery agencies. In Ontario, the common assessment tools are based upon the language of learning outcomes, and serve the purposes of "establishing the literacy levels of adults, identifying individual learner goals and competencies, measuring progress in learning activities, guiding program improvements and demonstrating accountability to funders" (Ministry of Training, Colleges, & Universities, 2000, p. 9).

LINKING COMPETENCY-BASED ASSESSMENT TO INSTRUCTION

Competency-based assessment, which requires learners to demonstrate skills, leads to competency-based instruction with its emphasis on the mastery of identified skills. Competency-based instruction is based on the assumption that literacy can be fragmented into a hierarchy of skills that must be mastered so the individual can be functionally literate in today's society. Individuals become "functionally literate" by mastering competencies within one level, and then moving up the ladder to the next level.

Figure 3.4 on the following page illustrates the performance indicators used in Ontario for interpreting text at Level One (the lowest level) and Level Five (the highest level). Interpretation of a text is broken down into two performance indicators at Level One and six indicators at Level Five. When the performance indicators set out in these tests inform instruction, Level One students may not be provided with opportunities to practice and develop many important processes and skills such as the ability to make inferences. The underlying assumption is that Level One students need to develop "lower level" skills before they can develop "higher level" skills. This assumption is contrary to research that indicates that Level One students are capable of making inferences in narrative and expository text (Campbell & Malicky, 2002). This type of lock-step approach is in contrast to the concept of a spiral approach, in which processes, skills, and concepts are revisited and developed to new levels of complexity and the text becomes increasingly more difficult as adults progress through literacy programs.

> ▶ Rather than using the term "competency-based education," many literacy educators use the term "outcomes-based education."

> ▶ Competency-based instruction is based on the assumption that literacy can be fragmented into a hierarchy of skills that must be mastered so the individual can be functionally literate in today's society.

Figure 3.4 • Read with Understanding for Various Purposes

	LEVEL ONE	LEVEL FIVE
Features	**Performance Indicators**	
Interpretation	• Expresses thoughts and feelings about stories and events. • Predicts what may happen in a story; revises or confirms predictions.	• Questions and evaluates ideas (e.g., when summarizing the main ideas). • Uses structural and visual elements of the text to make reasoned judgements. • Makes more complex inferences. • Recognizes social and cultural influence and bias in writing. • Compares and evaluates the organization and detail of different texts that represent the same topic or story. • Clarifies and broadens own point of view by examining the ideas of others; expresses a personal opinion based on increased understanding.

SOURCE: Ontario Literacy Coalition. (2000). *The level descriptions manual.* Toronto, ON: Author.

CRITIQUE OF COMPETENCY-BASED ASSESSMENT

> Competency-based curricula explicitly specify learning outcomes and performance criteria at a range of levels. Though flexible to a degree in implementation, these curriculum-driven, externally accountable programs are quite different in spirit and practice from the former responsive adult literacy provision. (Doherty, Mangubhai, & Shearer, 1996, p. 19)

Competency-based assessment is directly connected to outcomes or competency-based education. This is a seductive concept cloaked in terms such as "learner-centred," "participatory," "accessible," "collaborative," "outcomes-based," "goal-directed," "results-oriented," "relevant," "functional," "holistic," and "authentic." It is difficult to critique an educational approach that appeals to our common sense and humanistic values. Yet the uncritical acceptance of this approach is almost as disturbing as the approach itself.

This task- or performance-centred orientation is a show-and-tell approach that reflects Western society's major orientation towards production. When a high value is placed on production and "doing," a great deal is sacrificed in a literacy program. Activities that do not produce a tangible end-product—activities that fall under the rubric of "being"—are not given a high premium. Activities such as sharing, analysis, and reflection of experiences appear to have no place in a competencies matrix. Research has clearly shown that while educators place importance on doing, students want a balance between "being" and "doing" activities in the literacy classroom (Campbell, 1994).

Competency-based assessment and instruction for beginning readers cover functional, goal-directed activities such as reading bulletin board notices, labels, shopping lists, recipes, flyers, and schedules. The competencies matrices purport to focus on measurable skills that are *relevant* to life—*yet, are these activities relevant to everyone? And are they the only skills relevant to adult living?* Essentially, these matrices predetermine what it means to be functionally literate. Literacy and life are captured in a matrix that purports to apply to *all* literacy students, despite their diversity, their situations, their interests, and their goals for themselves and their communities.

Learners may leave these programs having gained the skills required to read a landlord's notice or a company policy. But a more critical question focuses on whether or not students have had opportunities to discuss the rights of tenants and employees. In addition, students educated in an outcomes-based approach may graduate from such programs without ever learning how to deal with critical issues such as the violence, racism, and poverty in their lives. How can educators and students find time to discuss and explore these issues in-depth, when the focus of instruction is directed towards the students' achievement of particular outcomes?

In essence, the primary goal of competency-based education is to produce individuals who can function in society rather than people who feel empowered to challenge and change the status quo. According to Sanguinetti (1994), "discourses of competitiveness and human capital theory challenge 'social justice' discourses; discourses of efficiency and competency-based training confront discourses of critical literacy, progressivism, and holistic, learner-centred pedagogies" (p. 3). A great deal of what is relevant to adult escapes the behaviourist perspective with which competency-based systems are aligned.

Since competency-based assessment is integrated into an accountability system, there is also the risk that data on student performance will be compared between programs. This could lead to provincial systems of rewards and penalties, with intervention strategies being established to introduce incentives for improvement. Although this sounds Orwellian, such practices are already present in Alberta.

As a case in point, Alberta Learning funds post-secondary institutions through a "performance envelope," a process whereby institutions receive financial rewards for their performance. The government of Alberta was the first province to establish a Key Performance Indicators program that obliged institutions to submit outcomes data in order to qualify for bonus increments to their base grants. Performance indicators include the level of students' satisfaction, the number of students who complete the program, and the number of students who gain employment after leaving the program.

If institutions and/or programs have signed performance-based contracts, where funds are linked to learner outcomes and program impacts such as achieving employment, there is a real possibility that programs may succumb to a process known as "creaming." This process occurs when programs prefer to admit students who are most likely to achieve the learner outcomes specified in the matrix and who will make steady progress, rather than admitting students who require special support and have difficulty showing gains (Wrigley, 1998).

Authentic Assessment

DESCRIPTION

Authentic assessment uses a wide range of texts and tasks to assess a student's literacy development, skills, processes, and current capabilities. The assessment tasks include interviews, **informal reading inventories**, miscue analysis, **retellings**, dialogue and response journals, checklists of learner goals, self-assessments, and **portfolio assessment**. Although many authentic assessment tasks focus principally on the student's ability to write, they are deemed to be a valid measure of reading because the assessment tools measure what they purport to measure; e.g., reading comprehension is measured by having the student construct meaning from written text.

BACKGROUND

"The term 'authentic assessment' has arisen as a contrast to standardized assessment forms that appeared antiseptic and disconnected to any reality but that of a particular culture of assessment with its roots in the days of early experimental psychology" (Murphy, Shannon, Johnston, & Hansen, 1998, p. 139). In the 1980s, the demise of behaviourism and the emergence of the social constructivist model of learning, with its emphasis on understanding reading as the active construction of meaning within a social context, saw the need grow for different forms and types of assessment. As the limitations of standardized tests became more apparent, so did the awareness of the need for assessment that better matched the emerging theory of reading.

Many educators sought assessment tools that mirrored their views about literacy education, reading instruction, and student-educator relations. What emerged was a type of assessment that was congruent with their views of the educational system, and that embodied the social and cultural nature of literacy, meaningful contexts, reflective practice, and diversity. This form of assessment was deemed "authentic" because it took into account the complexity of reading, the importance of validity and interpretation, and the manner in which it emphasized strengths rather than weaknesses. Finally, this form of assessment corresponded to educators' views of working with students because it supported active, engaged participation.

The extent to which authentic assessment was used by adult literacy educators in the 1980s is not documented. The first pieces of literature on authentic assessment in adult literacy were published in the late 1980s (Lytle, Belzer, Schultz, & Vannozzi, 1989; Lytle & Wolfe, 1989). In 1997, a survey was conducted to determine the extent to which authentic assessment was used in colleges and community-based adult literacy programs across Canada.[2] The findings indicated that *all* of the colleges were using standardized assessments, while 80 percent of the community-based programs were using authentic assessment tools.

LINKING AUTHENTIC ASSESSMENT TO INSTRUCTION

Authentic assessment tools are usually closely aligned with curriculum and instruction, and in many instances the lines between assessment and instruction are blurred. Following authentic assessment, academic content is integrated with issues meaningful to students and learning is anchored in real-life situations and problems. Authentic assessment goes hand in hand with social constructivist learning theory, which is built upon the idea that as readers interact with text they construct meaning against a background of their particular socio-cultural environment and experiences.

Authentic assessment focuses on the literacy process, whereas standardized tests view literacy as a product. By understanding the literacy processes a student uses to construct meaning from text, an educator can gain a better understanding of how to instruct the student. For instance, an educator can analyze a student's retelling to determine if the student makes inferences and synthesizes information when he/she reads. If the retelling does not contain any inferences, the student may need to learn how to "read between the lines."

> ▶ In the late 1980s and early 1990s, the term "learner-centered assessment" was commonly used, rather than the term "authentic assessment."

> ▶ Following authentic assessment, academic content is integrated with issues meaningful to students and learning is anchored in real-life situations and problems.

CRITIQUE

There are two disadvantages to using authentic assessment. First, educators who engage in authentic assessment gather reading material from relevant and authentic sources such as the home, the community, and the workplace. However, in the effort to gather "authentic" material, the degree of text difficulty may be overlooked or disregarded. Although the material may be authentic, students may be frustrated by its difficulty. Consider the caution labels on medicinal products as a case in point. The words, aside from being multi-syllabic, may be unfamiliar to students, and therefore difficult to predict. According to the **Fry Readability graph**, the following text has a readability level of grade 10.

> CAUTION: Do not exceed recommended dosage. A persistent cough may be a sign of a serious condition. If symptoms persist for more than a week or tend to recur, or are accompanied by a high fever, rash or persistent headache, consult a physician. Do not use for chronic cough, chronic lung disease, asthma, shortness of breath, or if you have diabetes, heart or thyroid disease,

high blood pressure, glaucoma or difficulty in urination due to prostate enlargement, if you are taking a prescription drug for high blood pressure or depression, or as with all drugs if you are pregnant or nursing, unless directed by a physician. Keep this and all drugs out of the reach of children. Do not take this product if you are hypersensitive to any of the ingredients. Store at room temperature (15 – 30 C).

Source: Whitehall® Robins. Extra strength Robitussin® cough and cold decongestant. Permission to reprint granted.

A beginning reader faced with reading this caution label would probably be very frustrated. When the educator is not aware of the readability level of the text, it is difficult to match students with the appropriate level of instructional materials on an ongoing basis. This does not mean that the educator must avoid the use of authentic reading materials simply because they may be beyond the students' current reading capabilities. The challenge facing the instructor is to develop useful pre-reading **schema** building activities that will enable students to read authentic text.

The second disadvantage is that many authentic assessments such as portfolios and informal reading inventories are time-consuming and difficult for educators to construct, administer, and/or interpret. Rather than simply tabulating scores, authentic assessment requires educators to draw on their background knowledge and experience in order to interpret the assessment data and identify patterns in the student's reading performance.

Professional development is one way to enhance and develop educators' understanding and interpretation of informal reading inventories and portfolio assessments. As well, on-line communications provide a venue for educators to post ideas, provide suggestions, and answer questions about authentic assessment. Provincial and state literacy coalitions and government offices are already promoting the use of this type of communication.

Types of Assessment for Adult Learners: Summary

It is apparent that these types of assessment are not mutually exclusive. For example, conclusions drawn from standardized test results can be supported by observing and interacting with students as they read various materials. The key, of course, is balance. The effectiveness of an adult literacy program often depends upon the educator's ability to balance the assessment and interpretation of the students' current capabilities with what are often complex political and social considerations, in order to design and implement a program that responds specifically to the students' literacy needs.

A fundamental tenet of such a balanced approach is that all students can learn and grow as readers. The emphasis falls on the educator's ability to build a program that responds to the students' needs as revealed through assessment, rather than on interventions designed to help the students compensate for deficiencies within themselves. Because such an approach runs counter to many commonly held beliefs about the source of reading problems encountered by adults, the next section presents a perspective on the role that labels play in instructional decision-making.

Assessment and Learning Disabilities

A QUESTION FREQUENTLY ASKED by adult educators is, "How can you tell if a student is learning disabled?" The answer to this question depends on whether one is a psychologist or an educator. Psychologists administer a battery of tests to determine whether an individual is learning disabled. One of the tests in this battery is usually an intelligence test such as the *Stanford-Binet Intelligence Scale* or the *Wechsler Adult Intelligence Scale-Revised*. Based on such tests, in order to be diagnosed as learning disabled, individuals need to meet four criteria. The individual must:

- Have average to above-average intelligence.
- Demonstrate a discrepancy between intelligence and achievement test scores.
- Demonstrate a discrepancy between achievement and age and ability.
- Have learning problems that are not primarily the result of visual, hearing, or motor disabilities; mental retardation; emotional disturbance; or environmental, cultural, or economic disadvantage.

Learning disabilities, as defined by The Learning Disabilities Association of Canada[3] (2002), have a neurological origin:

> *Learning Disabilities* refer to a number of disorders which may affect the acquisition, organization, retention, understanding or use of verbal or nonverbal information. These disorders affect learning in individuals who otherwise demonstrate at least average abilities essential for thinking and/or reasoning. As such, learning disabilities are distinct from global intellectual deficiency.
>
> Learning disabilities result from impairments in one or more processes related to perceiving, thinking, remembering or learning. These include, but are not limited to: language processing; phonological processing; visual spatial processing; processing speed; memory and attention; and executive functions (e.g. planning and decision-making).
>
> Learning disabilities range in severity and may interfere with the acquisition and use of one or more of the following:
>
> - oral language (e.g. listening, speaking, understanding);
> - reading (e.g. decoding, phonetic knowledge, word recognition, comprehension);

- written language (e.g. spelling and written expression); and
- mathematics (e.g. computation, problem solving).

Learning disabilities may also involve difficulties with organizational skills, social perception, social interaction, and perspective taking.

Learning disabilities are lifelong. The way in which they are expressed may vary over an individual's lifetime, depending on the interaction between the demands of the environment and the individual's strengths and needs. Learning disabilities are suggested by unexpected academic under-achievement or achievement which is maintained only by unusually high levels of effort and support.

Learning disabilities are due to genetic and/or neurobiological factors or injury that alters brain functioning in a manner which affects one or more processes related to learning. These disorders are not due primarily to hearing and/or vision problems, socio-economic factors, cultural or linguistic differences, lack of motivation or ineffective teaching, although these factors may further complicate the challenges faced by individuals with learning disabilities. Learning disabilities may co-exist with various conditions including attentional, behavioural and emotional disorders, sensory impairments or other medical conditions.

"Learning disabilities," according to this definition, is a broad term that can be applied to a myriad of learning difficulties.

Adult educators tend to use checklists as an initial screening device to determine if a student might be learning disabled. Figure 3.5 on the following page is an example of the types of questions asked on a screening checklist.

The checklists ask questions about an individual's physical, social, spatial, and cognitive skills in order to determine how a deficit in a particular domain can interfere with the individual's ability to function effectively. For instance, a person with spatial skill difficulty could have trouble interpreting maps or following instructions involving directions, such as finding one's way in an unfamiliar city. It is of more than passing interest to note that when I do a self-assessment using one of these checklists, I am invariably at risk for being learning disabled.

Literature is available for educators that provides instructional strategies and programs for working with students who have been diagnosed as being "learning disabled." However, there is inevitably a tenuous link between assessment and teaching strategies. This is because the assessment tools used by psychologists and most educators to diagnose learning disabilities do not provide the information needed to design an effective instructional program. A psychologist's assessment will provide information about the adult's intelligence level, and his/her performance on a reading test such as the *Wide Range Achievement Test* (WRAT) or the *Woodcock Reading Mastery Tests-Revised*.

Figure 3.5 • Screening Checklist

Do you have trouble...	ALMOST	NEVER	SOMETIMES	OFTEN
• understanding what is said to you				
• putting your thoughts in words when speaking				
• finding a particular word(s) when speaking				
• taking part in conversations				
• with reading				
• with math				
• with handwriting				
• with spelling				
• writing your thoughts on paper				
• understanding jokes				
• remembering what you see				
• remembering what you hear				
• organizing, planning or keeping track of things				
• paying attention or concentrating				
• knowing right from left				
• following oral or printed directions				

SOURCE: Learning Disabilities Association of Canada. (1999). *Destination literacy: Identifying and teaching adults with learning disabilities*. Ottawa, ON: Author. Permission granted to reprint.

The WRAT contains three sub-tests: reading, spelling, and arithmetic. The reading sub-test requires the student to name 15 letters and pronounce 42 words out of context. Reading ability is generalized from the individual's ability to pronounce words. Since the assessment does not provide information on how the student processes print and/or meaning, the recommendation cannot specify which word identification or comprehension strategies need to be taught.

Although the student may have been categorized as being "learning disabled," the diagnosis and resulting label itself provide little information that can be translated into programming decisions. In fact, the label may prove to be almost as debilitating as the diagnosis itself.

Labels

STANDARDIZED TESTS play a major role in the labelling of students because standardization means that the student's score is compared with a sample of others in the same grade or of the same age. The score indicates whether the student's performance is average, above-average, or below-average; or the degree to which the student deviates from the mean. The use of standardized tests to label students took root in the public school system in the early 20th century, and continues to be used by public school and adult educational systems.

> Do you remember being labelled in primary school? We were probably all labelled in some shape or form during our days in the public school system. Perhaps you were assigned to a specific learning group such as the "turtles" or the "robins." In this case, you would have been cognizant of your label. Or perhaps there was a notation in your cumulative file that labelled you as having "average" or "above-average" intelligence. If you were labelled, do you recall when and why it happened? How did the experience of being labelled effect you?

Labelling is a contentious issue that evokes heated discussions among affected parties such as educators, students, and parents. The two labels commonly applied to adults who have reading difficulties are "dyslexic" and "learning disabled." These labels serve a number of purposes that may support or hinder the literacy aspirations of both educator and student, depending upon how they are perceived.

Viewed from a critical perspective, labelling serves to categorize people, which is an act of exclusion. When people are excluded or marginalized, they may receive certain privileges. The privileges one receives for being "learning disabled" or "dyslexic" might be the right to access funding or special accommodations. The first privilege—the right to access funding—applies to public school system funding formulas, which stipulate that students must be identified as "learning disabled" before receiving funding for appropriate remedial assistance. The second privilege—accommodations—applies to public school *and* post-secondary institutions. In college or university settings, students who are labeled "learning disabled" as a result of a diagnostic assessment are often allowed accommodations such as extended exam time or a scribe.

In Canada, adult basic education and literacy students generally do not require the label of "learning disabled" in order to qualify for financial assistance and/or accommodations. For example, Canadian students who meet the provincial or territorial government's criteria are often eligible for some financial assistance for full-time upgrading; these criteria do not include being labelled "learning disabled." Further, adult basic education and/or literacy programs attempt to provide *all* students with the accommodations they need to learn to read and write. The students do not need to be labelled in order to receive specific accommodations. For example, a beginning reader's instructor acts as a *scribe* when they engage in language experience activities. A beginning reader receives this particular accommodation, regardless of how they are categorized or labelled.

If an adult basic education student is denied an accommodation, such as computer software with speech recognition capabilities, it is usually because of limited funds. Polson and White (2000) conducted a national study to determine the barriers that prevented programs from providing appropriate accommodations for adults. A survey was mailed to 1,098 adult basic education providers in the states of California, Kentucky, Pennsylvania, Arizona, New Mexico, Kansas, Georgia, Minnesota, and Mississippi. Of the 622 surveys returned, 555 (54 percent) were usable. Their findings revealed that the most prevalent barriers to providing accommodations were financially related factors such as limited budget and number of available staff.

If an adult basic education student does not receive any accommodations for being labelled "learning disabled" or "dyslexic," then the question must be asked, "What purpose do labels serve?" In the first place, labelling serves to divert attention away from deficiencies related to instructional programming for a label situates the reading "problem" within the individual, i.e., the student has a disability that needs to be "fixed." In addition, when the problem is situated within the individual, the significant contribution that systemic factors such as race and class, as well the role that political factors embedded in educational policies and procedures play in creating a student's reading difficulties, can be discounted or ignored. For example, there might have been a mismatch between the instruction the student received at critical stages of his/her formal schooling and the instruction he/she needed in order to become a reader. Usually such a student would be diagnosed as being "learning disabled" when, in fact, the true disability rested within the program to which the student was subjected. In many cases, specific programs have been developed to respond to the "special needs" of disabled students. The following section takes a closer look at some of the links between labels and instruction.

> ▶ A label situates the reading "problem" within the individual, i.e., the student has a disability that needs to be "fixed." In addition, when the problem is situated within the individual, the significant contribution that systemic factors such as race and class, as well the role that political factors embedded in educational policies and procedures play in creating a student's reading difficulties, can be discounted or ignored.

Linking Labels and Curriculum

PERHAPS YOU HAVE INTERVIEWED OR WORKED with students who have labelled themselves as dyslexic. For the general public, the term "dyslexia" has become a catch-all term to describe reading difficulties; the word often means "reading words backwards" or transposing letters. Because of the misconceptions surrounding dyslexia, it is worthwhile to discuss the definition and history of dyslexia, and approaches to remedial instruction that follows the diagnosis.

At the turn of the century, opthalmologists and physicians drew attention to individuals who could not read and coined their term "congenital word-blindness" (Morgan, 1896; Hinshelwood, 1917). In the 1920s, Orton, a neuropsychiatrist and pathologist, dropped the term "word-blindness" in favour of "strephosymbolia" (twisted symbols); this label was later amended to "developmental dyslexia," a term that is still widely used. Orton concluded that dyslexia was a functional brain disorder—the failure of one hemisphere to become dominant in the control of language. Orton believed that this disorder lent itself to remedial training.

The notion that dyslexia is a deviation in language development is reflected in the International Dyslexia Association's[4] (1998) definition:

> Dyslexia is one of several distinct learning disabilities. It is a specific language-based disorder of constitutional origin characterized by difficulties in single word decoding usually reflecting insufficient phonological processing abilities. These difficulties in single word decoding are often unexpected in relation to age and other cognitive and academic abilities; they are not the result of generalized developmental disability or sensory impairment. Dyslexia is manifested by a variable difficulty with different forms of language, including, in addition to a problem with reading, a conspicuous problem with acquiring proficiency in writing and spelling. (p. 4)

This definition is grounded in the bottom-up theory of reading, which contends that individuals learn to read by progressing through a linear, sequential series of skills. Instructional programs based upon this theory tend to emphasize word identification skills at the beginning stages of reading development, rather than comprehension, and tend to discount the way that readers use their personal knowledge as they read. The Orton-Gillingham program, developed by Samuel Orton and his colleague Anna Gillingham, is a case in point; this remedial program is based on the belief that learning to read is easier if the reader starts with small, isolated pieces of information.

Instructors who use the Orton-Gillingham method take an alphabetic approach in order to establish for the students the concept that words are built out of phonemic units. The instructor begins by introducing the letters of the alphabet systematically, using visual, auditory, and kinesthetic techniques. Students learn the sound that is associated with one letter, and how to write it, before proceeding to the next letter. Once the students have mastered the sound-symbol associations for a prescribed group of ten letters, they begin to blend them together into words such as "bat," "map," and "him." Students learn the elements of language (e.g., consonants, vowels, digraphs, blends, and diphthongs) in an orderly fashion. They then proceed to advanced structural elements such as syllable types, roots, and affixes. As students learn new material, they continue to review old material to the level of **automaticity.** Eventually, the instructor addresses vocabulary, sentence structure, composition, and reading comprehension in a similar structured, sequential, and cumulative manner (Gillingham & Stillman, 1979).

This method is appealing for a number of reasons: It is manageable, requiring only that the instructor follow the prepackaged, prescriptive directions; students advance through "reading" stages that are observable and thus amenable to testing and recording; and progress can be reported using numerical data, such as "grade level." Despite the fact that the Orton-Gillingham method is painfully slow and time-consuming, in some cases, it may meet the needs of particular students, depending entirely upon the assessed needs of such students. As it is designed as a response to the dyslexic label and not to the needs of particular students, it tends to paint all students with the same brush. As a consequence, every "dyslexic" student receives the same program treatment regardless of whether or not he or she needs it, a disconcerting and unproductive approach to say the least.

Conclusion

IN A BALANCED READING PROGRAM, assessment informs instruction. In choosing an appropriate tool for your program, you need to consider the purpose of the assessment, your experience and knowledge in reading and assessment, educational policies and context, and material constraints such as time and funding. In choosing and administering an assessment tool, you can also keep the following principles in mind.

> The primary purpose of a reading assessment is to provide literacy educators and students with information that is useful in promoting a student's *growth* in literacy.

A reading assessment has the potential to provide information about the student's educational history, goals, concepts, instructional reading level, attitudes, current capabilities, skills, and processes. This information can be used to develop responsive programs, design lesson plans, choose materials, and implement effective teaching strategies.

> Assessment methods are compatible with the educational approach used in the classroom, learning centre, and/or tutoring situation.

Assessment is clearly related to the goals and objectives of instruction. If a literacy program embraces goal-directed and outcomes-based programming, then competency-based assessment is recommended. It would not make sense, for example, to use only a standardized test if instruction is competency-based. If, on the other hand, the literacy program uses a participatory educational approach, then authentic assessment is appropriate.

> Reading assessment is multi-dimensional; the assessment tools use multiple measures in order to gather information about the complex nature of a student's literacy.

In order to obtain a profile of the student's goals, concepts, skills, and processes, the assessment includes more than one method. It would be a disservice to the student to use only a standardized test to assess his/her literacy development. A standardized test, for instance, provides a grade score for a student's comprehension. In order to gain insight into the reading processes students use to comprehend text, an informal reading inventory could also be administered. In addition, an interview has the potential to provide valuable information relating to a student's knowledge of the reading process. For example, a student's answer to the question "What do you do if you don't understand something?" can provide insights into how the student interacts with text.

> Assessment procedures use authentic and relevant tests and tasks.

By using assessment tools that utilize whole texts, educators can observe whether students can orchestrate meaning, language, and print cues to decode words. Educators can also gain understanding about the student's ability to comprehend text. If the assessment utilizes only lists of words, educators can only observe whether students use print cues to decode words.

In many post-secondary institutions, the intake assessment tool is a standardized test. Educators working in these settings can support the standardized assessment by observing and interacting with the students as they read authentic material in the classroom.

> The purpose and nature of the assessment is explicit and clear to the student.

Prior to being assessed, students are provided with an explanation of the purpose for the assessment, and how the information will be used. Adult students need to be reassured that reading assessment is not a "pass/fail" test; rather, it is the first necessary or essential step in helping them to become proficient readers. Educators who, as a first step, develop a comprehensive profile of the student's current capabilities are in a strong position to provide appropriate and effective instruction. When this assessment profile/information is shared and discussed with students, they are in a position to monitor their personal literacy growth from the onset to the completion of their programs. All students have a right to know the results of their assessment.

> The assessment process is continuous and includes initial, ongoing, and final assessment of learning.

The initial assessment usually is designed to provide educators with a snapshot of the student's capabilities that is tied to a time and place, while ongoing assessment provides an unfolding montage of reading patterns and behaviours. For instance, in the initial assessment, the teacher might observe that the student reads narrative text actively and is able to construct meaning from this type of text. As the teacher observes the student reading in different genres and engaging in different forms of response, ongoing assessment might reveal that the student has difficulty skimming and scanning text to locate information. Ongoing assessment is particularly important for the student, as he/she can learn how to assess his/her reading skills and monitor progress.

A second reason for engaging in ongoing assessment is to determine whether students are benefiting from instruction. In tutoring programs, the only way to determine whether the student is receiving the needed instruction is by periodically assessing the student's progress. Sometimes, the student's instructional reading level may not increase, though the assessment might show an improvement in other areas. For example, the student could be making better use of context clues to predict unknown words. If the assessment indicates the student has not been benefiting from instruction, it might be time to make an adjustment in the instruction.

> Interpretation of assessment results takes into account the cultural and personal histories of individuals.

The student's cultural and personal histories[5] may affect their comprehension of text. Some cultures, for instance, teach students to memorize text, rather than to make predictions and inferences. Or the topic of the passage might be unfamiliar to the student, given his/her cultural background. In both cases, the student's cultural history may affect comprehension. If the student is anxious or depressed, his/her short-term memory may be impaired; this could negatively affect the ability to comprehend text.

> Assessment is fair and equitable.

All students are given the same opportunity to perform equally well on a reading assessment. In order for this to occur, the nature and content of the assessment considers the student's race, culture, ethnicity, class, and gender. Bias in an assessment is often very subtle and difficult to detect because most biases are part of the perspective we bring from our cultural background. Assessments such as informal reading inventories, which provide options and choices for the student, can help to prevent bias. This type of assessment provides the student with an opportunity to select the passage he/she wants to read.

C H A P T E R   S U M M A R Y

Educational assessment is a term that is often associated with testing, sorting, categorizing, and evaluating students. It sometimes has strong emotional connotations, usually negative, for both students and educators. This chapter has reviewed the three forms of reading assessment that tend to dominate educational practice in North America. The pros and cons of each form of assessment were discussed in terms of definition, purpose, background, shortcomings, and linkages to curriculum. The need for educators to be aware of the purpose for which a particular assessment procedure was designed plays an important role in which tool is chosen. ❧

References

American Educational Research Association, American Psychological Association & National Council on Measurement in Education. (1999). *Standards for educational and psychological testing.* Washington, DC: American Educational Research Association.

Anastasi, A. (1988). *Psychological testing* (6th ed.). New York: Macmillan.

Bainbridge, J. & Malicky, G. (2000). *Constructing meaning: Balancing elementary language arts* (2nd ed.). Toronto, ON: Harcourt Canada.

Brown, J.I., Fishco, V.V., & Hanna, G. (1993). *Nelson-Denny reading test.* Chicago: Riverside Publishing Company.

Campbell, P. (1994). *Participatory literacy practices: Having a voice, having a vote.* Unpublished doctoral dissertation, University of Toronto, ON.

Campbell, P. & Malicky, G. (2002). The reading strategies of adult basic education students. *Adult Basic Education* (12)1, 3-19.

CTB/McGraw Hill. (1994). *Tests of adult basic education. Forms 9 & 10.* Monteray, CA: Author.

Crombie, D. (1988). Message. *Learning, 5*(1), p. 13.

Doherty, C, Mangubhai, F. Shearer, J. (1996). Assessment as an ongoing feature of the learning environment. In C.J. Joy & E. Christina (Eds.), *Adult literacy and numeracy: Assessing change.* Melbourne, Victoria: Language Australia Publications. (ERIC Document Reproduction Service No. ED 405 488)

Fox Lee, J. & Strohmaier, R. (2000). *Common assessment of basic skills (CABS): Initial assessment in 5 levels* (3rd ed.). Kingston, ON: Literacy Link Eastern Ontario.

Fry, E. (1977). Fry's readability graph: Clarifications, validity and extension to grade 17. *Journal of Reading, 21*(3), 242-252.

Gillingham, A. & Stillman, B.W. (1979). *Remedial training for children with specific disability in reading, spelling, and penmanship.* Cambridge, MA: Educators Publishing Service.

Hansen, J. (1998). "Evaluation is all day, noticing what is happening": Multifaceted evaluations of readers. In S. Murphy, P. Shannon, P. Johnston, & J. Hansen (Eds.), *Fragile evidence: A critique of reading assessment* (pp. 105-123). Mahwah, NJ: Lawrence Erlbaum Associates.

Harcourt Brace & Company and The Psychological Association. (1988). *Canadian adult achievement test.* Toronto, ON: Author.

Hiebert, E.H., Valencia, S.W. & Afflerbach, P.P. (1994). Definitions and perspectives. In S.W. Valencia, E.H. Hiebert, & P.P. Afflerbach (Eds.), *Authentic reading assessment: Practices and possibilities* (pp. 6-21). Newark, DE: International Reading Association.

Hinshelwood, J. (1917). *Congenital word-blindness.* London: Lewis.

International Dyslexia Association. (1998). *Perspectives* quarterly newsletter, (4).

Jones, J.E. (1994). Portfolio assessment as a strategy for self-direction in learning. *New Directions for Adult and Continuing Education* no. 64. pp. 23-25. San Francisco: Jossey-Bass Publishers.

Johnston, P. (1998). The consequences and the use of standardized tests. In S. Murphy, P. Shannon, P. Johnston, & J. Hansen (Eds.), *Fragile evidence: A critique of reading assessment* (pp. 89-101). Mahwah, NJ: Lawrence Erlbaum Associates.

Karlsen, B. & Gardner, E.F. (1995). *Stanford diagnostic reading test* (4th ed.). Toronto, ON: Harcourt Canada.

Kerka, S. (1995). *Techniques for authentic assessment.* Educational Resources Information Centre. (ERIC Document Reproduction Service No. ED381688)

Kerka, S. (1998). *Competency-based education and training: Myths and realities.* Educational Resources Information Centre. (ERIC Document Reproduction Service No. ED415430)

Learning Disabilities Association of Canada. (1999). *Destination literacy: Identifying and teaching adults with learning disabilities.* Ottawa, ON: Author.

Literacy and Basic Skills Section, Workplace Preparation Branch. Ministry of Training, Colleges and Universities. (1998). *Working with learning outcomes: A validation draft.* Toronto, ON: Author.

Lytle, S.L. & Wolfe, M. (1989). *Adult literacy education: Program evaluation and learner assessment.* Washington, DC: Office of Educational Research and Improvement.

Lytle, S.L., Belzer, A. Schultz, K., & Vannozzi, M. (1989). Learner-centred literacy assessment: An evolving process. In A. Fingeret & P. Jurmo (Eds.), *Participatory literacy education. New Directions for Adult and Continuing Education, no. 42,* pp. 53-64. San Francisco: Jossey-Bass Publishers.

MacGinitie, W.H. & MacGinitie, R. K. (1992). *Gates-MacGinitie reading tests* (2nd ed.). Chicago: The Riverside Publishing Company.

Madaus, G.F. & O'Dwyer. (1999). A short history of performance assessment: Lessons learned. *Phi Delta Kappan, 8*(9), 688 - 695.

Ministry of Education and Training. (1998). *Literacy and basic skills (LBS) program guidelines.* Toronto, ON: Literacy and Basic Skills Section, Workplace Preparation Branch, Ministry of Education and Training.

Ministry of Training, Colleges and Universities. (2000). *Common assessment in the literacy and basic skills program.* Toronto, ON: Literacy and Basic Skills Section, Ministry of Training, Colleges and Universities.

Morgan, W.P. (1896). A case of congenital word-blindness. *British Medical Journal, 2,* 1378.

Murphy, S., Shannon, P., Johnston, P. & Hansen, J. (1998). *Fragile evidence: A critique of reading assessment.* Mahwah, NJ: Lawrence Erlbaum Associates.

Ontario Literacy Coalition. (2000). *The level descriptions manual.* Toronto, ON: Author.

Pearson, P.D., Spalding, E. & Myers, M. (1998). Literacy assessment as part of new standards. In M. Coles & R. Jenkins (Eds.), *Assessing reading 2: Changing practice in classrooms* (pp. 54 - 97). New York: Routledge.

Polson, C.J. & White, W.J. (2000). Providing services to adults with disabilities: Barriers to accommodations. *Adult Basic Education, 10*(2), 90-99.

Rudner, L.M. (1994). *Questions to ask when evaluating tests.* Washington, DC: ERIC Clearinghouse on Assessment and Evaluation. (ERIC Document Reproduction Service No. ED385607)

Sanders, M. (2001). *Understanding dyslexia and the reading process: A guide for educators and parents.* Toronto, ON: Allyn and Bacon.

Sanguinetti, J. (1994). *Negotiating competence: The impact of teaching practice of CGEA.* Victoria, Australia: NLLIA.

Statistics Canada, Human Resources Development Canada, & National Literacy Secretariat. (1996). *Reading the future: A portrait of literacy in Canada* (Catalogue No. 89-551-XPE). Ottawa, ON: Author.

Thorndike, R.L., Hagen, E.P., & Sattler, J.M. (1986). *Stanford-binet intelligence scale* (4th ed.). Itasca, IL: Riverside Publishing Company.

Wechsler, D. (1981). *Wechsler adult intelligence scale – revised.* Toronto, ON: The Psychological Corporation.

Wilkinson, G.S. (1993). *Wide range achievement test - 3.* Wilmington, DE: Wide Range, Inc.

Wrigley, H.S. (1998). Assessment and accountability: A modest proposal. *Adventures in Assessment,* Volume 11. Boston, MA: SABES/World Education.

Woodcock, R.W. (1987). *The Woodcock reading mastery tests – revised.* Circle Pines, MN: American Guidance Service.

Notes

1. The numerals 9 and 10 refer to the latest version of the test.

2. This survey was conducted by Pat Campbell and Flo Brokop. It was mailed to 105 adult educators, and a total of 58 (55 percent) responded to the survey. Of these, 93 percent indicated that they used a reading test to assess students' skills. All of the college-based programs used a standardized test to assess reading, while the community-based programs used a variety of assessment tools. The community-based programs used primarily in-house developed assessment tools (42 percent), informal reading inventories (30 percent), or a combination of these two tools (8 percent). A smaller percentage of the community-based programs used standardized tests (19 percent). Interestingly, none of the respondents used portfolio assessment for intake and/or ongoing assessment.

3   This definition was adopted by the Learning Disabilities Association of Canada on January 30, 2002. Retrieved September 21, 2002 from the Learning Disabilities Association of Canada Web site: http://www.ldac-taac.ca/english/ldac.htm

4   The International Dyslexia Association used to be called the Orton Dyslexia Society.

5   Their personal history includes their current personal situation and their physical and emotional health.

CHAPTER FOUR

Word Recognition

Introduction

Think of the similarities between tradespeople and literacy educators. They both arrive at their worksite with a set of tools or strategies. Both tradespeople and educators know that there isn't one tool that can be used in every situation; rather, there are specific tools and strategies that are appropriate for use in particular situations. While a plumber may be faced with figuring out how to increase water pressure, an educator may be faced with a student who has difficulty reading unfamiliar words. Both use a similar process to solve the problem. First, they use their expertise and knowledge to analyze the situation and locate the likely root of the "problem"; second, they choose the appropriate tool(s) or strategies for working with the problem; and finally, they work toward a clearly defined solution.

During the past 18 years as an adult literacy educator, I have noticed the same questions being asked by literacy coordinators and tutors. Consider this frequently asked question: "What approach should I use—whole language or phonics?" This type of question reflects a desire to bypass analysis and dive right into the "solution." This chapter suggests that there are a number of critical questions that educators need to ask and answer before they proceed to possible solutions. The following questions, which are also frequently asked, reflect the understanding that students require instructional programs tailored to their needs: "How can I determine the best place to start my students' instructional program?" and "How can I determine the most appropriate approaches to best meet the needs of the learners?" These questions and others like them, which focus on uncovering, defining, and analyzing students' current skills, strategies, and general reading capabilities, will be addressed in this chapter.

The first section, "Miscue Analysis," describes a technique that provides a window into the student's reading process (Goodman, 1973) and explains how to record, analyze, and code miscues. The second section, "Reading Patterns," shows how educators can use miscue analysis to determine the student's reading pattern. Once an educator has identified the reading pattern, he/she will know the strategies that will best meet the needs of the learner. The strategies that complement each reading pattern are described in detail.

Miscue Analysis

Introduction

Whenever you ask a student to read something orally, you will probably notice that he/she makes errors. Take a minute to jot down some of the reading errors you have observed and then compare your list to the one in Figure 4.1.

Figure 4.1 • Common Oral Reading Errors

- Skips words
- Guesses words
- Inserts words
- Repeats words
- Mispronounces words
- Misses beginning and endings of words
- Reverses words

As a result of observing a student reading, an educator might write a report that discusses a student's oral reading errors. It might read: "Carlos sometimes leaves out words and sometimes inserts them when he reads. Sometimes, he mispronounces words. Although he corrects about 25 percent of his errors, his reading does not generally make sense." Although useful as a start, this type of report is very limited in that it does not fully inform the instructor how to teach Carlos. Simply knowing whether a student leaves out, inserts, or mispronounces words will not usually help an educator to select appropriate reading strategies. Educators need to probe further and dig deeper in order to determine why the student made the errors in the first place.

Kenneth Goodman (1969) devoted considerable research into why beginning or struggling readers make "errors" as they try to read. He concluded that the "errors" these readers make were really not errors at all. He observed that in their attempts to decode new or unfamiliar words, they were using language cueing systems inappropriately and thus, unproductively. He suggested that rather than making errors, these readers were "mis-cueing" and aptly termed their attempts **"miscues."** He further suggested that an analysis of a reader's miscues can reveal not only the reader's current capabilities to use language-cueing systems, but can also provide the foundation for a successful intervention or instructional program that responds to the reader's needs.

Language-cueing Systems

When educators engage in miscue analysis, they attempt to gain an understanding of the language-cueing systems the reader uses to process print. As mentioned in Chapter 2, readers mainly use three language-cueing systems: graphophonic, syntactic, and semantic as they attempt to read.

- The graphophonic system refers to the relationship between letters and sounds. The reader maps sounds onto symbols in order to come up with words that "sound and look similar to words in the text."

- The syntactic system, sometimes known as grammar, refers to the conventional structure or word order of sentences. When using this system, the reader uses syntactic or grammatical cues to identify unfamiliar words in order to come up with words that "sound right in the sentence."

- The semantic system refers to meaning. When using semantic cues, the reader uses meaning to identify unfamiliar words that "fit in with the rest of the sentence."

Fluent readers utilize all three language-cueing systems at the same time when they are identifying unfamiliar words. For example, read this sentence:

> Beavers spend most of their day building or fixing their lodge and dam.

Consider a scenario where a reader is unfamiliar with the word "building" and has difficulty reading it. Using *semantic* or *meaning* cues, the reader could read to the end of the sentence, and then combine his/her knowledge of beavers with other meaning cues such as, "fixing," "lodge," and "dam" to identify the unfamiliar word. The reader could then confirm his/her prediction by sampling the *graphophonic* or *print cues* in the word "building." If he/she predicted the unfamiliar word as "digging," he/she could check out the accuracy of the prediction by associating a sound with the initial letter "b" in building. If the reader substituted "dug" for "building" it would probably indicate that he/she is not making use of *syntactic cue* or *grammar cues*. Asking the question "Does this word fit in with the rest of the sentence?" may help the reader to recognize that the substituted word is ungrammatical. When readers make use of syntactic cues, they are using their unconscious sense of what is grammatically acceptable within a particular language community to identify words that fit in the sentence structure.

The following example illustrates what happens when a student relies on only one language-cueing system. Read the two sentences and compare the text with the student's rendition.

Figure 4.2 • Miscue Example

Text: "Take the ring," she said.
Student: "Talk the ring," she said.

The student substituted "talk" for "take." What does the miscue "talk" indicate? Do you think the student was trying to use print cues to sound out the word? Do you think the student was trying to use meaning cues to read the word? Or do you think the student was primarily relying on print and/or grammar cues? In the example shown in Figure 4.2, the student appears to be relying primarily on print cues to decode the word "take." Although an educator cannot plan an instructional program based on the analysis of one miscue, this particular example does indicate that, in this instance, the student was more concerned with print than meaning.

Recording Miscues

> Informal Reading Inventories (IRI) require readers to respond to comprehension questions following the reading. The reader's ability to answer the questions accurately is also factored into the assessment of the text's level relative to the reader's ability.

When engaging in miscue analysis, you record, code, and analyze the student's miscues based on reading text at the student's **instructional level.** Essentially, a text is considered to be at the reader's instructional level if the reader can accurately identify 91 to 98 percent of the words in the text. If the student reads less than 91 percent of the words accurately, the text is considered frustrational. If the student reads 99 percent or more of the words fluently, the text is considered to be at the reader's independent reading level.

Begin by selecting reading material at the student's instructional level—the reader should be able to reasonably comprehend the content of the material selected. Informal reading inventories, such as the *Canadian Adult Reading Assessment*, are usually an excellent source of passages. Good judgement is still required in order to ensure that the passages are appropriate for both student and situation. Two copies of the passage are needed—one for the student to read and one for you to record the miscues. The student reads the passage twice: the first time silently, which serves as a "warm-up" for the student, and the second time orally, during which you record the student's miscues. While learning how to record miscues, you might want to ask the student for permission to tape-record his/her oral reading to ensure accuracy.

A set of conventions for recording miscues has been developed so that assessments can be shared and understood among educators. Figure 4.3 demonstrates the conventions used for recording miscues. Following Figure 4.3 is a description of six common types of miscues: substitutions, omissions, additions, pronunciation, inversion, and repetition.

Figure 4.3 • Recording Miscues

The Piano Lesson

                      Piano
Joe saw an ad in the paper. It said, "Pianos for Sale - $199."

     great   *and*
"What a deal!" thought Joe. "I can buy a piano for $199. I can sell it for ten times
     ^
     That
as much! This is too good to be true!" Joe sent the piano company a cheque.
                                        to
                                      ^

                                                  small
Six weeks later, Joe got a small box in the mail. He opened the box. Inside, was a little

plastic piano.

                                            P —————————————
Joe got mad. He phoned the Better Business Bureau. The man on the phone asked Joe
—
for the name and address of the piano company. The address was only a post box

number.

                       and
The man checked his records. He told Joe that there was no record of the piano
                       ^

company.

                                            _*didn't* ✔
Joe was sad. He had lost a lot of money on a little piano. But he did learn a big lesson

—some things *are* too good to be true.

SOURCE: Campbell, P. & Brokop, F. (2001). *Canadian adult reading assessment*. Edmonton, AB: Grass Roots Press. Reprinted with permission.

Word Recognition   **65**

Substitution

There are several types of substitutions. A substitution occurs when a student says a word that is different from the printed word. Sometimes, the substitution is a non-word. The substituted word may be a longer or shorter version of the text word, depending on whether the student added or omitted a suffix.

Speakers of non-standard English may omit word endings. This is a reflection of dialectical differences and *should not be coded as a miscue*. For example, Vietnamese students may not pronounce the final consonant sound because few words in their language end with consonant sounds.

The substituted word is recorded above the text word, as demonstrated in the following examples.

       Piano

It said, "Pianos for Sale-$199."

       small

Inside, was a little plastic piano.

Omission

Circle the omitted word or phrase, as shown in the following example.

He (had) lost a lot of money on a little piano.

Addition

An addition occurs when the student adds a word or a phrase. Indicate the point of addition by a caret and write the addition above the text, as illustrated in the following example.

     great

"What a ⌃deal!" thought Joe.

Pronunciation

This occurs whenever a word is pronounced for a student. When a student does not attempt to decode a word, wait for five seconds, and then pronounce the word. Write the letter "P" above the text word that was pronounced, as indicated below.

                      P

Joe got mad. He phoned the Better Business Bureau.

Inversion

An inversion occurs when the student changes the order of words. Draw a curved line for inversions as shown in the following example.

"What a deal!" thought Joe.

Repetition

A repetition occurs when the student repeats a syllable, word, or phrase. Draw a line above the repetition as illustrated below.

The man on the phone asked Joe for the name and address of the piano company.

Recording Self-corrections

A self-correction occurs when a student rereads a word or part of the text. This behaviour is recorded by placing a check mark after the recorded miscue and a line is drawn above the word(s) that were reread, as demonstrated in the following example.

—— alive ✔

There is only one queen bee in a hive.

According to Clay (1993), "efficient self-correction behaviour is an important skill in good reading" (p. 32). When readers self-correct their miscues, they are using the language cueing systems to monitor their construction of meaning. As they are reading, they might realize the word they substituted, added, or omitted doesn't make sense and/or fit into the sentence. So, they are cued by the semantic or syntactic system to "fix things up." Usually readers self-correct "on the fly," although sometimes readers do pause, consciously assess the situation, and then apply fix-up strategies.

Analyzing and Coding Miscues

After you have recorded the miscues, you can analyze them and begin to consider which cueing systems the reader is relying on in this particular situation. Miscues are analyzed to determine the extent to which the student used graphophonic and semantic cues (print and/or meaning cues) to identify the word. This information will help you to decide whether to teach print-based strategies such as phonics and word families, or meaning-based strategies such as the cloze procedure.

In order to establish whether the student was using print and/or meaning cues to decode a word, two questions need to be asked for each uncorrected miscue.

- Does the miscue look like the text word?
- Does the miscue make sense in the sentence?

The answer to these questions determines how to code the miscue. Figure 4.4 illustrates how to code miscues, based on the answers to the two questions.

Figure 4.4 • Types of Miscues

TYPE OF MISCUE	Does it look like the text word?	Make it make sense in the sentence?
Print-based (PB)	Yes	No
Meaning-based (MB)	No	Yes
Non-Integrative (NI)	No	No
Integrative (I)	Yes	Yes

SOURCE: Campbell, P. & Brokop, F. (1996). *Supplemental training for practitioners in literacy education (STAPLE)*. Calgary, AB: Literacy Coordinators of Alberta.

If the miscue looks like the text word *and* makes sense in the sentence, it is an integrative miscue, and the letter "I" is written above the miscue. The passage in Figure 4.5 that illustrates the conventions for recording miscues appears here again. This time the miscues have been coded. Although self-corrections are *recorded*, they are not *coded* as PB, MB, I or NI.

In this next section, each type of miscue is defined and an example is provided. In addition, there is an explanation of how to analyze the miscue.

Figure 4.5 • Coded Miscues

The Piano Lesson

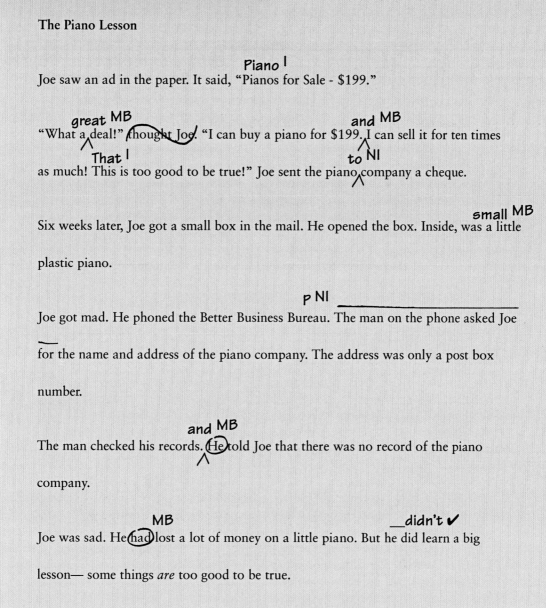

Joe saw an ad in the paper. It said, "Pianos for Sale - $199."
(Piano I above "Pianos")

"What a deal!" thought Joe. "I can buy a piano for $199. I can sell it for ten times
(great MB above "deal", and MB above "$199")

as much! This is too good to be true!" Joe sent the piano company a cheque.
(That I above "This", to NI above "piano company")

Six weeks later, Joe got a small box in the mail. He opened the box. Inside, was a little
(small MB)

plastic piano.

Joe got mad. He phoned the Better Business Bureau. The man on the phone asked Joe
(p NI above "phoned")

for the name and address of the piano company. The address was only a post box

number.

The man checked his records. He told Joe that there was no record of the piano
(and MB above "He")

company.

Joe was sad. He had lost a lot of money on a little piano. But he did learn a big
(MB above "had"; ___didn't ✔)

lesson— some things *are* too good to be true.

SOURCE: Campbell, P. & Brokop, F. (2001). *Canadian adult reading assessment.* Edmonton, AB: Grass Roots Press. Reprinted with permission.

A print-based miscue does not make sense in relation to the rest of the sentence. Instead, this miscue looks similar to the text word because it contains letters that are in the text word (see Figure 4.6).

Figure 4.6 • Print-based Miscue

bubble
Polar bears have a layer of blubber.

In Figure 4.6, the miscue "bubble" does not make sense in relation to the sentence. The text word "blubber" and the miscue "bubble" look similar. The miscue "bubble" contains six of the letters (b,u,b,b,l,e) that are in the text word "blubber."

To determine if a miscue is print-based, ask yourself:

- Does it look similar to the text word?
- Does it make sense in the sentence?

If the answer to the first question is yes and the answer to the second question is no, then it is a print-based miscue. In order to look similar to the text word, the miscue must contain one-half or more of the letters in the text word.

In order to make sense, the miscue must be meaningful in the sentence. If there is more than one miscue in a sentence, the sentence must be read as the student read it. For example, look at the two miscues in the following sentence:

mad   newspaper
Joe saw an ad in the paper.

These two miscues are print-based because they look similar to the text word, but do not make sense when the sentence is read as the student read it: Joe saw an mad in the newspaper.

MEANING-BASED MISCUE (MB)

A meaning-based miscue is defined as one that makes sense in the sentence but does not look similar to the text word. Although it does make sense in the sentence, it might change the author's intended meaning (see Figure 4.7).

Figure 4.7 • Meaning-based Miscues

EXAMPLE 1

                                                   and

The man started to lower himself through the skylight when suddenly (he) got stuck.

EXAMPLE 2

                                  log

The beaver uses his front paws to put the trunks and branches into place.

In Example 1, the student made two miscues. The first miscue—"and" for "when"—makes sense in relation to the sentence. The text word "when" and the miscue "and" do not look similar. The only letter they have in common is "n." The second miscue, which is the omission of the text word "he," makes sense in relation to the sentence. Since it is an omission, you assume that the reader did not use the print cues in the omitted word. In Example 2, note how the miscue "log" slightly changes the author's intended meaning. In this example, the miscue "log" is a meaning-based miscue as it makes sense in the sentence and does not look like the text word.

To determine if a miscue is meaning-based, ask yourself:

- Does it look similar to the text word?
- Does it make sense in the sentence?

If the answer to the first question is no and the answer to the second question is yes, then it is a meaning-based miscue. In order to make sense, the miscue needs to make sense within the sentence. Every miscue in a sentence needs to be read to determine if a single miscue makes sense within the sentence. For omission and additions, you need only ask "Does it make sense?" If the answer is yes, then it is a meaning-based miscue.

INTEGRATIVE MISCUE (I)

An integrative miscue occurs when the miscue makes sense in the sentence and is visually similar to the text word (see Figure 4.8).

Figure 4.8 • Integrative Miscues

EXAMPLE 1

cheaper.
It is chewy.

EXAMPLE 2

grind
Beavers use their sharp teeth to gnaw through the trunks of young trees.

In each example, the miscue looks similar to the text word because it contains one-half or more of the letters that were in the text word. Each miscue also makes sense in relation to the sentence.

To determine if a miscue is integrative, ask yourself:

- Does it look similar to the text word?
- Does it make sense in the sentence?

If the answer to both questions is yes, then it is an integrative miscue.

NON-INTEGRATIVE MISCUE (NI)

A non-integrative miscue occurs when the miscue is not meaningful and does not look like the text word. A word that you pronounce for the student is classified as a non-integrative miscue (see Figure 4.9).

Figure 4.9 • Non-integrative Miscues

EXAMPLE 1

man
Wild rice is a tall grass-like plant.

EXAMPLE 2

P
The children played with a wooden spinning top that is called a driedl.

In Example 1, the miscue "man" does not make sense, nor does it look similar to the text word "tall." In order to look like the text word, the miscue would need to contain two or more letters from the text word. In Example 2, the tutor pronounced the word "driedl" for the student. The student used neither print or meaning cues to decode the text word.

To determine if a miscue is non-integrative, ask yourself:

- Does it look similar to the text word?
- Does it make sense in the sentence?

If the answer to both questions is no, then it is a non-integrative miscue. As well, words that you pronounce for the student are classified as non-integrative miscues.

Reading Patterns

WHEN ALL OF THE MISCUES ARE CODED, a pattern will usually emerge. This is because most struggling readers tend to rely on the same language-cueing system(s) when they are reading material at their instructional level. An analysis of the miscues may indicate that the student generally relies on print cues to decode words. Once you have identified the student's miscue pattern as print-based, meaning-based, integrative, or non-integrative, you can make a decision as to the type of instruction he/she needs (Campbell & Brokop, 1994).

Print-based Pattern

When the majority (over 50 percent) of miscues are print-based, the students are relying too heavily on letters and sounds in order to identify unfamiliar words. These students need to learn how to use meaning cues, syntactical cues, and background knowledge to identify words. Figure 4.10 illustrates a student's print-based pattern. Note how the majority of the student's miscues look similar to the text word but do not make sense.

Figure 4.10 • Print-based Pattern

_{want PB}
She went into the pawn shop. She said, "I need some money." He said, "What can you   _{with PB}

_{rug I}
sell?" She showed him a ring and a watch.

_{p NI}
"Take the ring, " she said. "Are you sure?" he asked. "Yes, take it." The man took the

ring. He put it in a box.

_{give I}   _{thank PB}
Then the man gave the woman some money. He gave her $120. The woman took the
_{think PB}   _{bring PB   city PB}
money. Then the man gave the woman a ticket. The woman took the ticket. She began to cry.

Once you have determined that a student is a print-based reader, you can share the analysis with the student. The conversation could begin by asking the student, "What do you think good readers do when they come across an unfamiliar word?" A typical response from a print-based reader might be, "They try to sound it out." You can explain that good readers guess or predict words, along with trying to sound them out. The notion that "guessing" is "permitted" and encouraged may assist students in reconceptualizing reading; they may have equated guessing with cheating in the past. Readers' concepts about reading influence the way(s) in which they read; challenging these concepts may influence their literacy development.

STRATEGIES FOR RESPONDING TO PRINT-BASED PATTERN READERS

Think blank strategy

Have you noticed how print-based readers tend to read every single word in a piece of text? It might be necessary to discuss the characteristics of good readers, and to explain that reading every word is often not necessary in order to understand something. This is sometimes a new idea for adult readers to accept (Thistlethwaite, 1994). To reinforce this idea, Thistlethwaite recommends a "think blank" strategy. This entails encouraging readers to just "think blank" when they come to an unfamiliar word, and continue reading to the end of the sentence. After they have read the entire sentence, ask them to think of a word or words what would make sense in the blank. Then, they can attend to the first print cue in the unfamiliar word to see if it matches the first print cue in their prediction(s). According to Thistlethwaite, "often context plus knowledge of the sound of the initial consonant will be all that is needed for the reader to pronounce the word if the word is one that is in the reader's speaking vocabulary" (1994, p. 23).

> The think blank strategy may be difficult for English as a Second Language (ESL) students because the topic of the passage may be out of their realm of experience, and the unfamiliar word may not be part of their speaking vocabulary. A reader's background experience determines how much meaning the context can yield for him/her; an ESL student may find it difficult to use context to make a prediction. ESL students will probably need some prereading activities to build the their schema or background knowledge about the topic, and to teach new vocabulary. A good way to build the student's schema and vocabulary is to engage in "narrow reading." This is similar to theme teaching in that, over the course of several lessons, the student is presented with several pieces of text on the same topic.

Cloze procedure

If students have difficulty with thinking blank and skipping words, you can use the cloze procedure. This strategy forces the student to skip words because words have already been replaced by blank spaces! The term "cloze" is related to closure. The cloze procedure reflects our tendency to see things as a whole, even if parts are missing. It is an effective strategy to use with a print-based reader because it encourages a student to use his/her background knowledge, meaning cues, and grammar cues to predict the deleted word. The procedure involves the following steps:

- Photocopy a short, complete passage at the student's instructional reading level. Leave the first sentence intact so the reader can have some meaning cues. Delete some of the predictable words with white-out or Post-it notes. Figure 4.11 shows an example of a cloze passage created from *Fran's Story*.
- Explain the purpose of the exercise to the student; e.g., "You can use information from the story to figure out what the word might be. The word should make sense and sound right in the sentence." Demonstrate the procedure.
- Ask the student to read the passage and to make predictions. Encourage the student to read around the blank, thinking about the author's ideas that come before and after the blank.
- Discuss why and how the student selected certain words. If the student chooses an inappropriate word for the blank, ask "Does it make sense?" and "Does it sound right?" The question "Does it make sense?" helps the student to use meaning cues and the question "Does it sound right?" helps the reader to use grammar cues.

When teaching cloze, or any strategy, be sure to explain the purpose or rationale. Understanding the purpose will help the student to understand how this exercise differs from conventional fill-in-the-blank activities. It is good practice to affirm appropriate choices. For instance, the prediction "woods" rather than "forest" is an appropriate choice in the sentence "She went to pick blueberries in the forest." It is important not to insist upon an exact match between the author's words and the word offered by the student. Remember, the purpose of the exercise is not to achieve exact matches, but to have the student use grammar and meaning cues to predict words that make sense in the sentence and the text as a whole.

Figure 4.11 • Cloze Passage

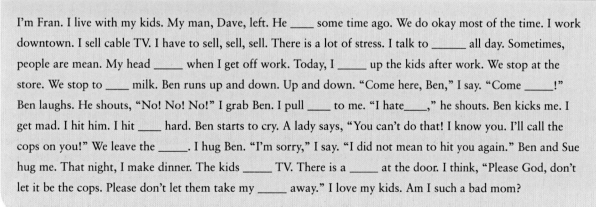

I'm Fran. I live with my kids. My man, Dave, left. He ____ some time ago. We do okay most of the time. I work downtown. I sell cable TV. I have to sell, sell, sell. There is a lot of stress. I talk to _____ all day. Sometimes, people are mean. My head _____ when I get off work. Today, I _____ up the kids after work. We stop at the store. We stop to ____ milk. Ben runs up and down. Up and down. "Come here, Ben," I say. "Come ____!" Ben laughs. He shouts, "No! No! No!" I grab Ben. I pull ____ to me. "I hate____," he shouts. Ben kicks me. I get mad. I hit him. I hit ____ hard. Ben starts to cry. A lady says, "You can't do that! I know you. I'll call the cops on you!" We leave the _____. I hug Ben. "I'm sorry," I say. "I did not mean to hit you again." Ben and Sue hug me. That night, I make dinner. The kids _____ TV. There is a _____ at the door. I think, "Please God, don't let it be the cops. Please don't let them take my _____ away." I love my kids. Am I such a bad mom?

SOURCE: Kovats, M. (2000). *Fran's story*. Edmonton, AB: Grass Roots Press.

Meaning-based Pattern

A meaning-based pattern is one in which the majority of the student's miscues are coded as meaning-based. Quite often, a meaning-based pattern contains a lot of omissions and additions simply because the reader is not paying close attention to print. Students with a meaning-based pattern rely too heavily on meaning context and their background knowledge to predict unfamiliar words. This sometimes results in a situation where the students' meaning is quite different from that intended by the author. Figure 4.12 illustrates a meaning-based pattern.

Figure 4.12 • Meaning-based Pattern

work MB
They stayed in the same job for twenty or thirty years. Their jobs didn't change too

How ✔ *very* MB *easy* MB
much. Now things are different. High school is not enough. If you want a good job, you

are MB *changing* I
have to go to college or university. Also, jobs often change because of technology and

new ideas. You need to learn new things constantly just to keep your job. These days

a MB
you can't count on having one job for your whole life.

In order to gain a reasonable grasp of the writer's intended meaning, this type of reader needs to pay more attention to print (letters and sounds associated with them) and word structure (word parts), while continuing to think about the meaning. If the student has been identified as a meaning-based reader, you might want to engage in a discussion to increase the student's awareness about his/her reading behaviours. In order to ground the discussion in a real-life example, the student's oral reading could be tape-recorded and then played back. While listening, the student could circle the words he/she substitutes and omits. This would serve to heighten his/her awareness that he/she would benefit from paying more attention to print and word structure. Be sure to praise the student for his/her ability to produce meaningful miscues.

Four strategies that assist meaning-based readers in focusing on print and word structure are word families, word sorts, word blitzing, and **structural analysis**.

Word families

The word family strategy encourages students to look for familiar patterns in unfamiliar words and develops their ability to generalize from the known to the unknown. A word family consists of words that rhyme and contain the same word pattern or common cluster of letters. For example, "ake" is a common word pattern, and its word family consists of "make," "take," "lake," "fake," and "bake," etc. Prerequisites for developing word families are the ability to rhyme and the knowledge of consonant sounds, blends and digraphs. As students become more proficient with this strategy, they might enjoy finding exceptions to regular sound-symbol "rules" (for example, look, cook, fool, school).

One possible source for words is the student's word bank. A word bank consists of a file box and index cards, with each index card containing one word. These words are ones which may have been studied during previous lessons; they may be taken from books, language experience stories, documents, or signs. Some students might also prefer to keep a copy of their word banks in their notebooks.

The words that are selected from the word bank need to contain a common word pattern. The words in Figure 4.13 are taken from a machine tool operator's word bank; only the bolded ones would be appropriate for the word family approach. The word bank is a useful or effective way of keeping track of words the student can recognize by sight. By using sight words for word family instruction, the student can concentrate on analyzing the words into parts rather than trying to decode them letter by letter.

Figure 4.13 • Machine Tool Operator's Word Bank

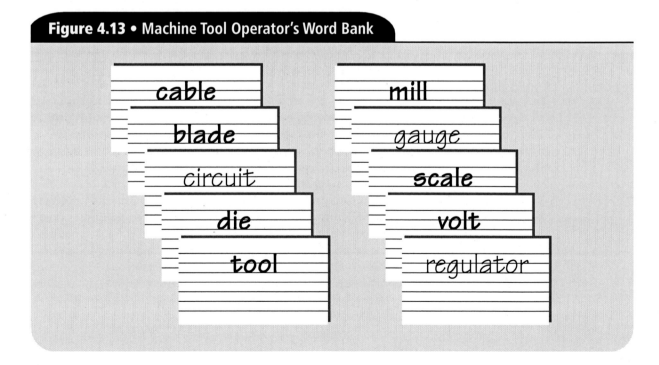

Figure 4.14 • Word Pattern

ight
sight
bight
fight
right
tight
*height

Begin instruction by asking the student to read the word and pronounce the sound of the first letter. Then, ask the student to pronounce the rest of the word. If the word was "sight," the student would read the word, then pronounce "s" and "ight." Next, print the letter pattern "ight" at the top of the page, and list the word "sight" underneath it. Ask the student if he/she can think of another word that looks and sounds the same. These words can be added to the list. If the student suggests a word that sounds the same but has a different word pattern, use an asterisk to indicate that it is spelled differently (see Figure 4.14).

If a student was reading the paragraph in Figure 4.15 and was unable to pronounce the bolded words, the word family strategy would be an appropriate approach to teach the words "shade" and "right."

Figure 4.15

Majestic **shade** trees lined the jogging path where Karen ran each evening. Randomly placed benches were often occupied by seniors with their pigeon companions, but today a young man caught Karen's **attention** by the strange way he sat, face **uplifted** to the sky. His **right** hand rested upon the huge head of a German shepherd.

Structural analysis, described next, provides a strategy that is appropriate for teaching the multi-syllabic words "attention" and "uplifted."

Structural analysis

As students encounter more difficult reading material, they are required to decode multi-syllabic words. Structural analysis refers to the identification of words using larger, more meaningful units than simply letters (Bainbridge & Malicky, 2000). Instruction in structural analysis focuses on the following units: compound words, roots, prefixes, suffixes, and syllables.

To informally assess whether students have an understanding of the concept of structural analysis, you can ask them to verbally list the different ways they know to figure out unfamiliar words. The list might include "asking someone," "reading ahead and then going back and putting in a word that fits," "sounding it out" or "thinking of a word that looks and sounds the same." If the list doesn't include a response such as "breaking the word into parts" you can point out that breaking words into "syllables" or "chunks" will can also help them to identify longer unfamiliar words.

To begin instruction, select some familiar words and write several sentences, using the words in context (see Figure 4.16). Read each sentence out loud, accentuating the syllable breaks (e.g., I was *search ing* for a *bar gain* in the *fly er*.) This will help the students to "hear" the syllables. After the sentence has been read, present the words with the syllable boundaries shown. This will help the students to "see" the syllables. It is important for students to see the relationship between oral and written syllables.

Figure 4.16 • Structural Analysis Activity

I was **searching** for a **bargain** in the **flyer.**
search • ing   bar • gain   fly • er

The **baby** turned red in the face and **started** to cry.
ba • by   start • ed

The dog was **whining because** it **wanted** to go **outside.**
whin • ing   be • cause   want • ed   out • side

She bent down to **untie** her **shoelace.**
un • tie   shoe • lace

When the students understand the concept of syllables, you can ask them to read the words from their word bank, accentuating each syllable. If a student has difficulty, place your hand under your chin and ask him/her to do the same in order to experience how one's chin drops down for each spoken syllable.

When the students have mastered the art of hearing syllables, teach the generalizations that can be used to break words into syllables (Tarasoff, 1999):

- Each syllable contains one vowel sound.
- Prefixes and suffixes generally form separate syllables.
  (walk • ing, un • lock)
- A compound word is divided between the two words that form the compound. (shoe • lace)
- Double consonants or two consonants together are divided, except in the case of blends and digraphs. (bas • ket) (rath • er) (blan • ket)
- A single consonant between two vowels often goes with the second vowel. (o • pen)
- The consonant before "le" usually begins the last syllable. (can • dle)

The students often need lots of practice in structural analysis before they feel confident about their ability to divide words into syllables. When students encounter an unfamiliar multi-syllabic word in a passage, encourage them to use both structural analysis and context to identify it. It's important to stress that for the purpose of breaking words into syllables there are some general guidelines, though no clear-cut right or wrong ways. Students should also be encouraged to experiment with vowel sounds. In the word "untie" (un • tie), the student might pronounce the "u" in "un" with a long vowel sound, resulting in a nonsense word. If this happens, simply ask him/her to try again using a different vowel sound. Once the students have figured out a word using structural analysis, they should check to make sure the word makes sense in the context of the sentence.

Word sorts

Word sorts enable students to discover similarities in words rather than being told or shown how they are alike (Gillet & Temple, 1994). You can ask students to classify, compare, contrast, and sort words according to their print (patterns, prefixes, suffixes, syllables) or sound features. The words that are used in sorting activities can be drawn from the student's word bank.

There are two types of word sorts: an open sort and a closed sort. It is best to begin with a closed sort activity, as it requires convergent thinking, making it easier than an open sort, which requires divergent thinking. In closed sort exercises, the sorting criterion is stated in advance. You might ask the student to find words that end in a suffix, contain a silent "e," or have the same word pattern as "lake." Students then search for words in their word bank that meet the criterion. In an open sort activity, the sorting criteria are not stated in advance. The student is presented with word cards and asked to sort them according to how they sound or look. As an extension, the students can explain the criterion or rationale that they used to sort the words.

Word blitzing

Word blitzing (Fagan, 1990) helps a meaning-based reader pay more attention to print while continuing to think about the meaning. This activity works well in a group or tutoring context. To begin instruction, have the student(s) brainstorm words on a topic meaningful and relevant to their lives. Figure 4.17 shows a sample list for the word "photography."

As you record the words, you might want to describe the structure of some of them. For instance, you could explain that "snapshot" is a compound word as it contains two words. You could then ask the students to perform a similar analysis or observation of the other words in the list. Once the students have reviewed their brainstormed lists of words, they can be asked questions about the meaning of the

Figure 4.17 • Photography Word List

camera	film
light	snapshots
expensive	negatives
model	instant
pictures	flash
develop	colour
wedding	pose
photographer	photos

words; for example, Which three words mean the same? Then, they can be questioned about word structure. Sample questions for the words in Figure 4.17 might be "Which words are plural?" "Which words contain a suffix?" "Which word contains the most syllables?" The lesson can end with the students adding the words they have learned to their word bank. The students can be encouraged to copy the words syllable by syllable, rather than letter by letter, as the former technique is faster and helps them process larger units of print.

Non-integrative Pattern

A non-integrative pattern occurs when the majority of miscues do not make sense and do not look similar to the text word. A person with this type of pattern usually has a rate of reading that is painstakingly slow. Quite often, this type of reader waits for the instructor to pronounce words. A non-integrative pattern indicates that the reader has developed few strategies for dealing effectively with print. Consequently, this type of pattern is more prevalent among beginning readers than among intermediate or advanced readers. Figure 4.18 illustrates a non-integrative pattern.

Figure 4.18 • Non-integrative Pattern

p NI   kings NI   read NI
It takes time to lose body fat. The key is to exercise and eat right. You need to exercise at least

there PB   joy PB   sane NI
three times a week. Ride a bike. Go for a jog. Go for a swim. Walk the dog. Run up and

down the stairs.

p NI
You should change the way you shop and eat. Look for fat-free foods in the store. Cut out the

p NI
candy and chips. Load up on fish, grains, and fruit. Soon, you will begin to look slim and trim.

If a student has not learned effective strategies for decoding print, it is important to provide familiar language and repetitive reading experiences. Non-integrative readers need to be taught how meaning, grammar, and print cues can help them to predict unfamiliar words. These three cueing systems can be applied only within the context of "whole text." If a student is presented with lists of words to read, he/she will be able to use only print cues. The non-integrative pattern reader needs to be taught through a variety of strategies such as language experience, word families, word sorts, cloze procedure, sight words, phonics, and minimal cue messages.

Language experience

Language experience stories provide the student with familiar and meaningful text that is highly predictable and easy to read. Language experience is an integrated writing-reading-discussing activity in which the instructor records a student's or group of students' dictated story or personal anecdote. Figure 4.19 is an example of a language experience story. This approach works well with individuals or in group settings. Language experience creates a link between the reader's spoken and written language, making it particularly effective for ESL students or those who speak a nonstandard variety of the language. These students may have difficulty identifying words in conventional materials that use standard English.

Figure 4.19 • Language Experience Story

My Daughter's Camping Trip

My daughter went on a camping trip for four days. She had quite the time. She had lots of fun. They tipped over the canoe. They were frozen. I was so happy to see her home again.

Language experience begins by discussing a topic of interest with the student(s). Conversations could revolve around current events; the student's job, family, goals, dreams, or hobbies; a childhood experience; a recent excursion or field trip; or a favourite television show. Photographs of family members or friends could be used to elicit memories, or photographs from magazines could jump-start interesting thoughts and ideas. If you are working with a group, you might want to focus on serious topics that are significant to the students and their lives. You could find a "**code**" (object, drawing, poster, sign, flyer, film) that represents problems, issues, or concerns that have been raised by the students.[1] A picture of a male doctor talking to a female patient might be a suitable code for a group of women who do not feel confident talking with professionals. The purpose of the code is to provide a stimulus so that students can clearly see the issue or problem, emotionally respond to it, critically reflect on it, and take action in regard to it (Freire, 1970, 1973; Wallerstein, 1983).

When using language experience for the first time, you might encounter some hesitation or resistance from the students. Students might compare the way you are teaching them, with the way in which they were taught in grade school. If the students were used to learning from a set of readers or workbooks, they will probably be expecting the same type of instruction from you. If the students feel uncomfortable voicing their opinion about your teaching methods, they may experience anxiety and frustration. It is important for you and the students to discuss each other's expectations and for you to explain why you are using language experience.

In some instances, you might find that the students do not feel comfortable discussing or sharing personal matters. If this is the case, you can ask the students to select a piece of text that contains information they want to learn. The text could be a set of instructions, information about a medical condition, or a newspaper article. You can read the text to the students, and then engage in a discussion based upon what you have read.

After the discussion, ask the students to dictate the story, so that you can record it. Record what the students dictate in print rather than cursive handwriting. Print is usually easier to read and is closer to what the student will see in books and other text. It is important that the students watch you print and read each dictated word in order to establish the link between oral and written language. If you are working in a one-to-one setting, be sure to sit beside, and not across from, the student so that the student can read what is being written.

There is an ongoing debate about honouring the student's language as you record the ideas. Let's say the student dictated this sentence: "Dat is the way we do it and we ain't gonna change." How would you scribe that particular sentence? Would you change "dat" to "that," "ain't" to "are not," and "gonna" to "going to"? Or would you accurately record the words in order to establish the link between oral and written language? I would recommend that you record the student's dialect, which may include non-standard English or ungrammatical structures, but use standard spelling. I would suggest scribing the sentence in the following manner: "That is the way we do it and we ain't gonna change." If you change the student's dialect, the student may begin to feel judged. In addition, changing the student's dialect alters the voice and tone of the what the student said; rendering it in standard spelling does not. This is particularly important if students are taking their dictated writing home to share with others who may not be familiar with the processive nature of language experience learning.

After the dictation, read the story to the student, and then read it with the student. You may want to point to the words or trace them across the page in order to develop the students' ability to eye-voice match. Invite the student to read the story independently. For a repetitive reading experience, the dictated story can be read over and over again. Although you may find this tedious, the student will benefit by frequent exposure to the same piece of text. Through the process of repeated reading, the student gains confidence in his/her fluency and can begin to put different interpretations on the same text. In addition, by frequent rereading, students begin to automatically identify words and phrases; and thus they develop a bank of sight words. As students begin to match memorized words with the print, they also begin to gain implicit phonics knowledge. As they develop their sight vocabulary, they begin to use contextual and graphophonic cues more effectively; subsequently, the need to use predictable, repetitive, or familiar language texts in the instructional program decreases.

Sight words

A sight word is a printed word that a person can immediately recognize because it is stored in the visual memory. It is estimated that fluent readers recognize 99 percent of the words they read by sight (Bainbridge & Malicky, 2000). In order to develop non-integrative readers' fluency and reduce word-by-word decoding, they can be encouraged to develop their repertoire of sight words.

For beginning adult readers, it is important that their sight word vocabulary contain words that they encounter at home, work, and in the community. Social sight words, such as "fire exit," "bank," and "open" are words that students frequently encounter outside the home; knowing these words might make the student feel more at ease in the community, and more confident in a formal educational setting. High-frequency sight words are those that occur repeatedly and constitute about 50 percent of the words in any piece of text; knowing these words will help to increase the student's automaticity when they are reading. The *Dolch* word list (1942), which categorizes 220 words according to grade level, is an example of a high-frequency word list (see Figure 4.20).

Figure 4.20 • Dolch Pre-primer Word List

a	and	away	big	blue	can	come	down	find	funny
for	go	help	here	I	in	is	it	jump	little
look	make	me	my	not	one	play	red	run	said
see	the	three	to	two	up	we	where	you	yellow

Although the list was first published in the 1930s, it has repeatedly been found to be relevant and useful in more recent materials (Burns, Roe & Smith, 1999). However, it does contain a few words, such as "play," "jump," and "run," that are probably more frequent in children's books than in those read by adults. Personal sight words, such as "Jenny," "simmer," and "corrosive" are words that students want to learn because they are related to their jobs, interests, or home lives; knowing these words might increase the student's sense of independence. Quite often, language experience stories are a good source of personal sight words.

There are several ways to develop, study, and review the student's sight word vocabulary. For the look, cover, write, and check method, ask the student to choose five words. These can be high-frequency words, personal words, social sight words, or words from a language experience story. The student looks at the word, covers it, writes the word, and uncovers it to check the spelling. As the student looks at the word, ask "Do you see something in this word that will help you to remember it?" This question serves to focus the student's attention on the visual features of the word.

You can also ask the students to keep lists of words that they have difficulty reading or spelling. These words can be printed on index cards, and the sight word can be illustrated on the back of the card. This technique enables students to study independently. When they can't read the word, they can simply flip over the card for a reminder. When they can read the word, they can flip over the card for confirmation. Word bingo is an enjoyable way to reinforce the students' sight word vocabulary. It is the same as regular bingo, except that sight words are used rather than numbers.

Phonics

Phonics is an instructional system based on the relationship between letters and their spoken sounds. The two major approaches to phonics instruction are the **analytic approach** and the **synthetic approach.** The analytic approach proceeds from whole to part; that is, a student is presented with a word and is then taught the association of sounds to letters and letters clusters within the word. In the synthetic approach, the student is taught the sounds that are associated with individual letters or letter clusters. The student is then taught how to blend the sounds together to form words.

Rather than teaching phonics by a predetermined sequence (consonants, vowels, blends), you can determine the extent of the student's phonics knowledge through observation. The student may already know several consonants or have a well-developed knowledge of consonants but have difficulty matching the appropriate sound to vowels. If this is the case, you are off to a good start because consonants carry most of the surface structure meaning load. For example, compare sentences 1 and 2.

1. Sh_ w_nt t_ th_ SPC_ _nd f_ _nd h_r d_g.

2. _ _e _e_ _ _o _ _e _ _ _ A a_ _ _ou _ _ _e_ _o_.

Note how sentence 1, which doesn't contain vowels, is easier to read than is Sentence 2 which doesn't contain consonants. Quite often, educators are concerned when students can not master the vowel sounds. Yet, this example strongly suggests that it is more important for students to learn consonants.

To begin analytic phonics instruction, present the student with one of his/her sight words that begins with a consonant or consonant blend he/she needs to learn. Using a sight word to introduce the letter(s) and sound enhances learning by moving from the familiar to the unfamiliar, from the concrete to the abstract, and from the whole to the part. After presenting the sight word, try following these steps:

- Ask, "What can you tell me about the sound you hear at the beginning of this word?"
- Ask the student to think of other words that begin with the same sound. This can be a difficult task for some students.
- Ask the student to look through his/her sight word bank to find the words beginning with the sound on which you are focusing.

- Say several words and ask the student to identify those beginning with the sound you are teaching.
- Say several words and ask the student to identify those which end with the sound you are teaching.
- Ask the student to create words by joining the sound/letter to a list of letter units. For example, if the student is learning the letter "m," ask him/her to make words with these letter units: "ake," "ade," etc.

These steps, which require the student to engage in visual and auditory tasks, are quite different from workbook exercises, which have a heavy focus on visual tasks. Workbook exercises are also questionable because they teach phonics in a predetermined sequence. Laubach literacy programs use a workbook called the *Voyager Foundation Book* (1999). This workbook, which is intended for beginning readers, teaches phonics in the following sequence: consonants, short vowels, consonant blends.

Some students find themselves in instructional settings that use the synthetic phonics approach. The student is taught the sounds for individual letters and letter clusters and is encouraged to apply this knowledge when he/she comes across an unfamiliar word. After the student has sounded out each letter or letter cluster, he/she has to blend the sounds to make the word. The synthetic phonics approach requires students to learn rules; unfortunately, most phonic rules turn out to have so many exceptions that they have little reliability as rules. Thistlethwaite (1994) reviewed the literature on phonics rules and found that many rules are not consistent or reliable (see Figure 4.21).

Figure 4.21 • Reliability of Phonics Rules

RULE	RELIABILITY
When two vowels go walking, the first one does the talking.	97% reliability for "oa" 65% reliability for "ea" and "ai" unreliable for "ei," "ie," and "oo"
Silent "e" rule The short vowel sound becomes a long vowel sound in a consonant-vowel-consonant word when "e" is added to the end of the word.	63% reliability
Hard "g", soft "g" rule When "g" is before "a," "o," or "u," it has the hard sound; and when it is before "e," "i," and "y," it has the soft sound.	64% reliability

Rather than teaching the rules, Thisthethwaite recommends that students be taught to consider alternative pronunciations. Let's say the student is trying to figure out the word "fail" in this sentence:

If your brakes fail, try pumping the brake pedal.

Encourage the student to try several pronunciations ("fale," "fell," "feel") and to use the one the makes sense in the sentence.

> ▶ The notion of "transfer" plays a key role when you are working with ESL students. If the student's first language contains patterns similar to those found in English, it can result in a positive transfer because the literacy skills developed in the first language transfer to the second language (Lighthouse & Spada, 1993; Rivera, 1999). If you are teaching phonics to English as a Second language students who are literate in their first language, ask them about the correspondence between letters and sounds in their language. If there is no correspondence, you will have to teach the concept of a sound/symbol relationship. Chinese, for example, is a symbolic language in which the symbols or characters reflect meaning rather than sounds.

Minimal cue sentences

Minimal cue sentences, an adaptation of the cloze procedure, can be used to encourage adults to use both meaning *and* print cues to decode unfamiliar words (Campbell & Brokop, 1996). Rather than deleting whole words, delete a portion of the word (initial consonant, ending, vowel digraph) upon which the student needs to focus. The following sentence is from a language experience story in which the suffix was deleted, and replaced with dashes.

We went hunt _ _ _ on the weekend.

When presenting the sentence to the student, ask what cues can be used to unlock the minimal cue sentence. After the sentence has been completed, discuss whether it is possible to read without knowing all the vowel sounds.

Integrative Miscue Pattern

This pattern occurs when many of the miscues are coded as integrative, and/or there is a balance of meaning-based and print-based miscues. Some of the miscues will be self-corrected, indicating that the reader is monitoring his/her comprehension (see Figure 4.22).

Figure 4.22 • Integrative Miscue Pattern

sheriff's | room MB
The FBI agent burst into the chief's office.

striking ✔
"We've got them! Baker, Maffie, Pino—the whole stinking lot. O'Keefe confessed

can't | chasing ✔
everything. I cannot believe how good these crooks were. They were casing the

the |
building, making plans, walking in and out of that place for two years. They knew

and ✔
everything—security systems, schedules, who turned what light on when. You want to

get |
know how they got inside?

tartered PB
The agent flipped through his tattered notebook.

An integrative miscue pattern indicates that the student uses a combination of print, context clues, and background knowledge to identify unfamiliar words. Once the student has identified the word, he/she confirms the prediction by seeing if it makes sense in the rest of the sentence or passage. If the word does not make sense, the student might make a second attempt at predicting the word. This type of reader possesses a variety of strategies for decoding unfamiliar words. Although this pattern is indicative of a good reader, the student will still need to engage in extensive reading in order to achieve automaticity and become a fluent reader.

Automaticity is the ability to carry out a complex act rapidly and without conscious awareness or control (Bainbridge & Malicky, 2000). Achieving automaticity in reading can be compared to achieving automaticity while driving a car with a standard gear shift. When you first start driving a standard, the journey is rough and jerky as you have not mastered the art of shifting gears. Gradually, through practice, you think about shifting gears at an unconscious level, rather than at a conscious level. Once you have achieved automaticity, your attention can move away from trying to shift gears in a seamless fashion to more important matters such as driving defensively. When readers achieve automaticity, they can recognize words effortlessly and focus their attention on more important matters such as constructing meaning from text.

C H A P T E R   S U M M A R Y

The focus of this chapter has been on the strategies that readers use to identify and read words fluently. The principal aim of word recognition instruction is to develop the struggling reader's awareness of the strategies that proficient readers use, usually without conscious effort, to identify unfamiliar words. Proficient readers rely on three language-cueing systems to identify words: graphophonic or print, syntactic or grammar, and semantic or meaning. Instruction in word recognition strategies is most productive when it is based on close observation and assessment of the cueing systems adult readers use as they read. A diagnostic assessment can be done by recording and coding the miscues that the reader makes while reading out loud. When all of the miscues are coded, a pattern will usually emerge.

A reader generally exhibits one of four general miscue patterns: print-based, meaning-based, integrative, or non-integrative.

- A print-based pattern is evident when the majority of the reader's miscues look similar to the text word but do not make sense.
- A meaning-based pattern is demonstrated when the majority of the reader's miscues make sense, but do not look similar to the text word.
- A non-integrative pattern is demonstrated when the majority of the reader's miscues do not make sense and do not look similar to the text word.
- An integrative miscue pattern is demonstrated when the reader uses a combination of print, context clues, and background knowledge to identify unfamiliar words.

Readers who demonstrate any of the preceding patterns can benefit from direct strategy instruction designed to develop their ability to use the three language-cueing systems in an integrated and balanced way. Adults will also benefit if the following keys are kept in mind:

☞ The first key to success is to match the instructional strategy to the adult's needs as a reader. This means that thorough assessment and analysis precedes program planning and implementation.

☞ The second key to success is to develop the student's conceptual awareness of the reading process. By discussing and focussing on the strategies used by proficient readers, the student develops awareness of how such readers used the cueing systems to identify words fluently and automatically.

☞ The third key is to ensure that the reading material used for instruction is as close as possible to the adult's instructional reading level.

☞ The fourth key is to combine word recognition strategy-building with application in authentic and relevant contexts. This means that opportunities for shared and individual reading are part of the planned program activities.

In a balanced approach, word recognition is one cornerstone of an instructional program. Another cornerstone relates to the ways that readers construct meaning from the text. This aspect, commonly referred to as comprehension, is the focus for the next chapter. ❧

References

Bainbridge, J. & Malicky, G. (2000). *Constructing meaning: Balancing elementary language arts* (2nd ed.). Toronto, ON: Harcourt Canada.

Burns, P.C., Roe, B.D. & Smith, S.S. (2002). *Teaching reading in today's elementary schools*. New York: Houghton Mifflin.

Campbell, P. & Brokop, F. (1996). *Supplemental training for practitioners in literacy education (STAPLE)*. Calgary, AB: Literacy Coordinators of Alberta. Distributed by Grass Roots Press.

Campbell, P. & Brokop, F. (2000). *Canadian adult reading assessment*. Edmonton, AB: Grass Roots Press.

Clay, M.M. (1993). *An observation survey of early literacy achievement*. Portsmouth, NH: Heinemann.

Dolch, E.W. (1942). *Basic sight word test*. Champaign, IL: Garrard.

Fagan, W.T. (1990). *The L-I-T-E-R-A-T-E program: A resource book for literacy instructors*. Edmonton, AB: University of Alberta.

Freire, P. (1970). *Pedagogy of the oppressed*. New York: Seabury Press.

Freire, P. (1973). Education for critical consciousness. New York: Seabury Press.

Gillet, J.W. & Temple, C. (1994). *Understanding reading problems: Assessment and instruction* (4th ed.). New York: HarperCollins College Publishers.

Goodman, K.S. (1969). Analysis of oral reading miscues: Applied psycholinguistics. *Reading Research Quarterly, 5*, 9-30.

Goodman, (1973). Miscues: Windows on the reading process. In K.S. Goodman (Ed.), *Miscue analysis: Applications to reading instruction* (pp. 3-14). Urbana, IL: ERIC and NCTE.

Kovats, M. (2000). *Fran's story*. Edmonton, AB: Grass Roots Press.

Lighthouse, P. & Spada, N. (1993). *How languages are learned*. Oxford: Oxford University Press.

Rivera, K. (1999, December). *Native language literacy and adult ESL instruction*. ERIC Digest. Washington, DC: National Center for ESL Literacy. Retrieved August 10th, 2002 from the ERIC Digest Web site: www.cal.org/ncle/digests/natlit2.htm

Siedow, M.D. (1999). *Voyageur: Reading and writing for today's adults. Voyaguer foundation book*. Syracuse, NY: New Readers Press.

Smith, F. (1983). *Essays into literacy*. Exeter, NH: Heinemann.

Tarasoff, M. (2000). *Reading instruction that makes sense: Black line masters*. Victoria, BC: Active Learning Institute.

Thistlethwaite, L.L. (1994). Phonics-one important piece of the pie: A holistic perspective. *Adult Basic Education*, *4*(1), 19-34.

Wallerstein, N. (1983). *Language and culture in conflict*. Don Mills, ON: Addison-Wesley Publishing.

Notes

1   Chapter Six provides more information on using codes.

CHAPTER FIVE

Comprehension

Introduction

> They struggled through Blake's *Songs of Innocence* and *Songs of Experience*, Samuel Richardson's *Clarissa, or the History of a Young Lady*. They read *Paradise Lost*. She saw much in the poems and stories that he did not. She was sometimes cryptic and high-minded in a way he found off-putting. She could wander into flights of speculation beyond his interest or understanding... (Crummey, 2001, p. 42)

If you've ever attended a book club meeting, the lively discussion and debate act as a reminder of how the interpretation of a piece of literature is dependent upon one's knowledge, experience, and assumptions, as well as one's social and cultural values. Since comprehension is dependent on the interplay of three factors—the reader, the text, and the context—the interpretation of text will inevitably vary from person to person. The first section of this chapter, "Factors Affecting Comprehension," discusses the influence or contribution that the reader, the text, and the context has on or makes to the construction of meaning.

The second section, "Comprehension Patterns," explores the processes readers use to construct meaning from text. Readers tend to use different processes or approaches to construct meaning from text. Some readers are able to provide the gist of a story, but may be unable to recount any of the details. In contrast some readers, if asked, are able to answer all of the "who," "what," when," and "where" questions but may be unable to draw inferences from their reading. This section explains how educators can develop an effective instructional program based on the ways in which the reader interacts with text.

Factors Affecting Comprehension

The Reader

Struggling readers sometimes attribute their comprehension difficulties to a weak memory, yet these same individuals can effectively remember and juggle most aspects of their lives, perhaps indicating a well-developed memory for significant events and information. If memory is not their primary problem, why do some students have difficulty comprehending text? In this section, we will explore how active reading and knowledge of content, text structure, and strategies affect readers' ability to comprehend what they read.

ACTIVE READING

Imagine that you are curled up in bed reading *The Handmaid's Tale* by Margaret Atwood. You are determined to finish the chapter despite your exhaustion. As you turn to look at the bedside clock, you realize you can't remember anything from the two pages you just read. Does this scenario sound familiar? Even fluent readers sometimes become disengaged with the text due to fatigue, stress, or distractions.

The following activity illustrates what is meant by the phrase "being an active reader." As you read the excerpt from the book *She's Come Undone* in Figure 5.1, make a list of any significant thoughts that enter your head while you are reading.

Figure 5.1 • She's Come Undone

From the beach, she had looked black, but now, swimming beside her, saw that her skin was mottled, blotched with darker and lighter grays. I reached out to touch her. She felt firm and muscular against my palm, my shaking blue fingers. Against my lips. The kiss was soft and coarse. Salty.

I swam underwater to the front of her and resurfaced, bobbing and treading water. I was weightless.

Her massive head and snout were covered with knobs—ugly, patternless bumps littered with barbed chin stubble, sharp to the touch. Her scarred mouth gaped open, as if she'd died trying to drink her way back to safe, deep water. Her jaw, half above the surface, half below, was lined with thick broom bristle. Her eyes were underwater.

I held my breath and went under, my own eyes open.

The eye stared back at me without seeing. This iris was milky and blank, blurred by sea water. A cataract eye, an eye full of death. I reached out and touched the skin just below it, then touched the hard globe itself.

This was how I could die. This was where.

SOURCE: Reprinted with permission of Atria Books, an imprint of Simon & Schuster Adult Publishing Group, from SHE'S COME UNDONE by Wally Lamb. Copyright© by Wally Lamb.

Think back to the strategies you used or what you thought about as you read this excerpt. What did you consider to be significant? Since this is a piece of fiction, you might have employed strategies such as visualizing, self-questioning, clarifying, predicting, inferring, and monitoring your comprehension. In contrast, when you read non-fiction, you probably employ a different set of strategies such as identifying and retaining main ideas and important details, and summarizing in order to remember or recall information.

Research indicates that fluent readers actively engage with the text, using a variety of strategies. Researchers have used the think-aloud strategy as a way of understanding the strategies and processes that readers use subconsciously or unconsciously as they read. Pressley and Afflerbach (1995) assembled and reviewed over 40 research studies that used the think-aloud strategy, to access the cognitive processes used by fluent readers. In each of the studies reviewed, individuals read texts, and as they did, they verbally reported what they were thinking. Pressley and Afflerbach concluded:

> Good readers are selectively attentive. They sometimes make notes. They predict, paraphrase, and back up when confused. They try to make inferences to fill in the gaps in text and in their understanding of what they have read. Good readers intentionally attempt to integrate across the text. They do not settle for literal meanings but rather interpret what they have read, sometimes constructing images, other times identifying categories of information in text, and on still other occasions engaging in arguments with themselves about what a reading might mean. After making their way through text, they have a variety of ways of firming up their understanding and memory of the messages in the text, from explicitly attempting to summarize to self-questioning about the text to rereading and reflecting. (p. 79)

It is clear that from this review of the research, that fluent or proficient readers actively employ, either consciously or unconsciously, many different strategies and procedures as they read. It is also apparent that in most cases, struggling adult readers are unaware of how they can become actively engaged in their own reading. A useful instructional strategy designed specifically to heighten students' awareness of the strategies fluent readers use to comprehend text is the think-aloud strategy.

Think-aloud strategy

This strategy utilizes the modelling process—the teacher verbalizes his/her own thoughts while reading a passage orally, so that students will realize how and when to do the same. As the passage is read, the students read the same passage silently and listen to the teacher's self-commentary. Davey (1983) recommends that the passage "contain points of difficulty, contradictions, ambiguities, or unknown words" (p. 45). Figure 5.2 provides examples of think-alouds for the excerpt from *She's Come Undone,* a novel by Lamb (1992).

Figure 5.2 • Examples of Think-alouds

Make predictions and develop hypotheses.

"From the title, I think it will be about a woman who goes crazy."

"I think it is about some sort of large fish, perhaps a whale."

"I think the water must be really cold, because her hands are blue and shaking."

Describe visual images.

"I can see the water. It is dark blue and calm. The fish is close to the shoreline."

Share an analogy or make a link with prior knowledge.

"This reminds me of the time I went swimming in the ocean. The water was so salty and cold."

Identify and monitor a confusing point.

"This part is confusing, what does "hard globe" mean? Perhaps as I read on it will become clear."

"I don't understand this part. I will have to go back and check before I read on."

Engage in self-correction or use fix-up strategies.

"I need to reread this paragraph. I'm not sure if the fish is dead or alive."

"Perhaps if I read on, I'll understand better."

After a few modelling sessions, the student works together with a partner to practice think-alouds, using a short passage.

The students can also practice independently by using the checklist in Figure 5.3. Ask students, as they read, to place a check beside each strategy as they are aware of its use. At the end of the reading, students can tally up the checkmarks. This information enables students to identify their preferred approach or response to reading.

Figure 5.3 • Checklist for Think-alouds

STRATEGIES	Not very much	A little bit	Much of the time	All of the time
Predicting				
Visualizing				
Making links				
Monitoring problems				
Self-correcting				
Using fix-up strategies				

SOURCE: Davey, B. (1983). Think aloud–Modelling the cognitive processes of reading comprehension. *Journal of Reading 27*(1), p. 46.

This section discussed the importance of active reading. It is evident that "meaning, learning, or any kind of synthesis of experiences may not arise at all until the reader has entered into—and become [actively] engaged with—the story world" (Enciso, 1992, p. 100). The next section explores how readers' prior knowledge affects their comprehension.

PRIOR KNOWLEDGE

> The many active processes of reading—predicting, construction of images during reading, monitoring of comprehension and rereading, summarization, and interpretation—depend greatly on *prior knowledge,* with skilled reading being an articulation of prior knowledge and these active reading processes. (Pressley, 2000, p. 551)

Fluent readers automatically and without conscious effort activate their prior knowledge about the subject matter of a particular text to understand what they are reading. The relationship between prior knowledge and reading comprehension has long been recognized by researchers and practitioners. Two researchers, Wilson and Anderson (1986), summarized a decade of research on the role of prior knowledge in comprehension. They reported that "the knowledge that a reader brings to a text is a principal determiner of how that text will be comprehended, and what may be learned and remembered" (p. 32). The extent of this knowledge influences the quality of a reader's understanding.

Schema theory is an explanation of how people store their knowledge, how they learn, and how they remember what they have learned (Anderson & Pearson, 1984). This theory suggests that knowledge is stored in memory and packaged in units called schemata.[1] There are schemata for situations, events, actions, and sequences of actions; and schemata for concepts like "card" or "cheat."

People select a text because it suits their purpose; that purpose is the stimulus that activates their schemata or knowledge structure(s). As they are reading the text to fulfill their particular purpose, they are continually matching the text information with their schemata. If the text information does not fit with their *originating* schemata, they disregard the information that does not fulfill their purpose. As they select or identify useful information that is suited to their purpose, they rearrange their original schemata accordingly. The text information that matches or provides new insight into the original schemata is incorporated to form an expanded or revised schemata; this schemata is then applied to continued reading of the text. This is also known as *learning*.

Although it is seldom in real life that we chose to read material about which we have little or no knowledge or schemata, the following activity is designed to provide an insight into the way a reader's schemata may be activated during reading. As you read the following excerpt, make a note of the schema or knowledge structures that you activate.

> A long solid suit in dummy that is ready to run will frighten the typical defender. Instead of calmly assessing the true situation, he's likely to panic, frantically cashing whatever tricks he might have. Today's West became our latest victim.
>
> *Source: Wolff, B. (2002, January 14). The aces on bridge.* Edmonton Journal, *p. C5.*

Which words and phrases activated your schema? *Very* experienced card players have an elaborate "card game" schema that includes different types of card games such as bridge, mah jong, cribbage, and canasta. Reading the word cues "suit," "dummy," "tricks," and "West" serves to activate their "bridge" schema, likely permitting an inference that the excerpt is about a card game. Experienced card players might read the word cues "suit," "dummy," and "tricks" and not understand the significance of the word "West." They would probably still infer that the excerpt is about a card game. Readers who have no pre-existing "bridge" schemata, might read the word and phrase cues "ready to run," "frighten," "defender," and "victim" and activate an inappropriate schema such as "conflict." As you can see from this example, a reader's comprehension is affected by the breadth and depth of his/her schema(s) and his/her ability to use cues to activate the appropriate schema.

A major challenge faced by adult literacy educators lies in choosing instructional material that is authentic and relevant to students. Often the choice of authentic reading materials, such as government forms, training manual material, or essays and writing that critique social conditions, may be a necessary element or critical component of the instructional program. Unfortunately, the students may not be familiar with the form and content of the material and may not have the developed the schemata needed for active comprehension. In addition, because adult basic education students usually come from diverse backgrounds, the breadth and depth of knowledge and experience will vary. In such situations, it is critically important to engage students in prereading activities designed to help them develop the schemata they will need to construct meaning as they read.

Semantic mapping and K-W-L are instructional strategies designed to develop and activate students' schemata before reading expository text, particularly when students may not be familiar with the content. These two activities work well in a classroom or group setting because students have an opportunity to share their wealth of experiences and knowledge.

Semantic mapping

Semantic mapping or webbing is a technique used to create a visual display of relationships between the central concept in a text and related or supporting ideas (Pearson & Johnson, 1978). The visual display helps students see how single words or phrases can show how supporting concepts are related to both the main concept and to one another. During the process of constructing a semantic map, you can identify the extent of the students' prior knowledge about the central concept.

Semantic maps can be completed individually, in small groups, or with the whole class. When students complete their own maps, they can compare and contrast their completed maps with one another in order to expand and deepen their understanding of the concept.

Prior to the lesson, you need to determine the central concept of the text that the students have chosen or been assigned to read. For example, the central concept of the text in Figure 5.4 is colic.

Figure 5.4 • Colic Passage

One in ten babies gets colic. Babies who are three or four weeks old may get colic. It can last two months.

Babies with colic cry a lot. They can cry for one to two hours. They get red in the face. They pass wind. Colic will not harm the baby.

There are many ways to treat a child with colic. You can give him a bath. You can hold him in your arms. You can put a warm cloth on the child's tummy. You can hold him while you rock in a chair. You can take him for a car ride. You can place him in a wind-up swing. There is no cure for colic.

To begin the lesson, draw an oval on the blackboard, an overhead transparency, or a piece of paper. The concept "colic" is written in the oval, so that all of the students can view it. Semantic mapping begins with a brainstorming session in which students are encouraged to think of as many words as they can that are related to the central concept. At the end of the brainstorming session, these words can be sorted into categories, and a label can be generated for each category. This information can be used to construct a semantic map that illustrates relationships between categories (see Figure 5.5). After the text has been read, the class can revise the map by adding new knowledge and deleting words that were not related to the concept.

Figure 5.5 • Semantic Map

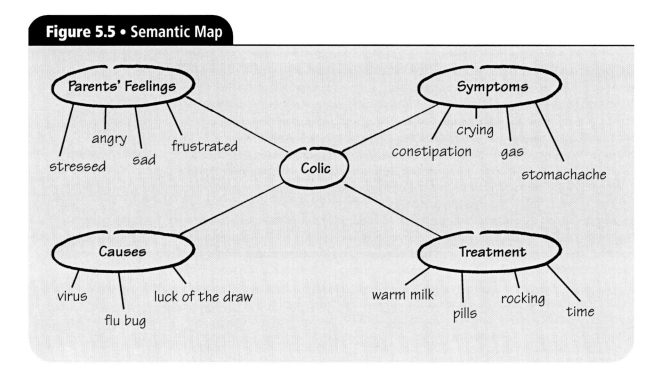

After constructing a semantic map about colic, students can participate in follow-up activities such as the ones described below.

- Students divide into groups and make up "quiz" questions relating to colic. Teams alternate questions, and a scorekeeper keeps score. The team responding to the question cannot refer to the "map" for the answer. The objective of this activity is to demonstrate to students how semantic maps enable them to remember key ideas and connections.

- Pairs or groups of students are given the same piece of text. You and each pair or group construct a semantic map on chart paper. When the maps are completed, they are posted on the wall. The teams discuss which supporting concepts can be collapsed. The objective of this activity is to encourage students to differentiate between key supporting ideas and "decoration"—ideas that are not really essential.

K-W-L (Know, Want to know, Learn)

K-W-L provides a framework to elicit readers' background knowledge and interest prior to reading expository text, in order to set a purpose for reading and help readers reflect upon their reading (Ogle, 1986). This activity requires you to facilitate three basic steps:

1 Access the students' prior knowledge.

2 Determine what they want to learn.

3 Recall what they learned as a result of reading.

These three steps can be visually displayed on a chart presented on the blackboard or an overhead transparency. Figure 5.6 is an example of a partially completed K-W-L chart on the topic "colic."

Figure 5.6 • K-W-L

K What We Know	W What We Want to Learn	L What We Learned
Babies cry	Is there a cure?	
Only some babies get colic	Is it contagious?	
Colicky babies get gas	How do babies get it?	
	How can you help your baby feel better?	

Before reading, the students' prior knowledge can be activated by having them brainstorm what they know about the topic or central concept. The students' responses are recorded in the first column, "What We Know." After the brainstorming session, students are encouraged to generate questions they would like answered about the topic. These questions are recorded in the second column, "What We Want to Know." After the group discussion, the students record their personal questions individually. As they pose questions, students set a purpose for reading the text. Once the students have developed their questions, they are ready to begin reading the expository text. As they are reading, students record the answers to their questions in the "What We Learned" column and make a note of the questions that still need to be answered. After students have completed their independent work, they come together as a group to discuss possible resources for finding answers to unanswered questions. For example, they might engage in further reading or bring in a guest speaker or search the Internet for information relating to the topic or concept.

METACOGNITION

Students often approach every reading task the same way, rather than selecting strategies based upon the nature of the task. Consider the following scenario, which illustrates the importance of knowledge about tasks and strategies. Many years ago, I interviewed a man who was frustrated by his inability to read all of the work memos that passed across his desk. Every night, he went home with a pile of unread memos, which his wife helped him read. Through discussion, we realized that he was reading the memos very slowly and carefully, rather than skimming and scanning them for key ideas, such as, dates, deadlines, meeting times, contacts, and pressing issues.

Skilled readers begin with a defined or definite purpose for reading in mind, and subsequently are aware of the demands of a reading task and the reading strategies needed to meet those demands. They use this knowledge to support and monitor their comprehension. This awareness and self-monitoring is generally referred to as metacognition. Figure 5.7 outlines key aspects of metacognition; each aspect is accompanied by examples of questions and/or statements that a reader may ask.

Figure 5.7 • Aspects of Metacognition

Aspect	Self-monitoring Prompts/Questions
Knowledge of abilities	What do I already know about this topic? Can I read and understand this?
Knowledge relating to the task	Why am I reading this? How difficult is it?
Knowledge relating to strategy use	How can I locate the information I need? What's the best way to study this?
Self-monitoring reading strategies	I don't understand. I'm going to reread this.

Fluent readers continuously monitor their understanding and when they feel that they are losing meaning, they apply "fix-up" strategies such as rereading, referring to purpose, reviewing key ideas in the text, or reconsidering the text's underlying structure in order to "fix" the reading problems they encounter. When educators ask students "What do you do if you don't understand something?" the students' response often reveals the extent of their metacognitive awareness. A response such as "I reread it" indicates that the student has a strategy in place for monitoring and evaluating his/her ongoing comprehension. A response such as "I don't know" indicates that the student might not be aware of the importance of constructing meaning or might not know how to engage in "fix-up" strategies when he/she does not understand something. In working with students, it is important to teach them when, how, and why to monitor their comprehension.

KNOWLEDGE OF TEXT STRUCTURES

When you go to your favourite supermarket, you likely carry a list in your hand and a visual map of the store in your head. You know that produce is to your far left, while dairy products are to your far right. Other food products are organized in a systematic fashion, making them easy to locate. If plum sauce is the first ingredient on your list, you can reasonably expect that it will be shelved in Aisle 2, along with the other Chinese food ingredients.

Texts and supermarkets are similar in the way that they utilize patterns of organization. Authors tend to organize their text, and grocery store managers their products, according to some plan or structure. Knowing the floor plan of a grocery store allows you to shop efficiently, while knowing the structure of a text helps you to navigate through the text in order to construct meaning. Moreover, awareness and knowledge of structure help readers and shoppers make predictions. By knowing the layout of a grocery store, you can locate a food item. Readers use their knowledge of different text structures in conjunction with story content to generate predictions and construct meaning (Pappas & Pettegrew, 1998).

On a daily basis, people are bombarded with written information at work, at home, and in the community. Just think of the written material that you may have skimmed, scanned, or carefully read recently—flyers, menus, newsletters, websites, e-mails, memos, editorials, movie reviews, recipes, fictional literature, contracts, and schedules. Your knowledge of and experience with the structure of these different written materials helps you to locate information, make predictions, and generally construct the meaning that you require.

When you hear the phrase "once upon a time," what kind of story do you expect will follow? If you responded "a fairy tale," you were using your knowledge of text structure. This knowledge provides readers with a set of expectations about the story, enabling them to anticipate what will be in the story. For fairy tales, these expectations might include that the number three will be predominant, as there are usually three wishes, three sisters, or brothers, or three events to test the hero or heroine's inner resolve or character. Why do you think that narratives like fairy tales are often easier for young children to comprehend and recall than expository text? For the past three decades, studies have shown that narratives are easier for children to understand because the content is more directly related to their experiences and prior knowledge. Researchers also contend that some children are more familiar with the temporal unfolding of narrative text structure as many of them have been brought up listening to stories (Rumelhart, 1977).

Adult literacy students may have a similar restricted knowledge of expository text structures usually because of their limited exposure to and experience with this type of text. Ideally, text structure should reside in the mind of the reader as well as in the text. Instruction in how to read the different types of expository text structures would be beneficial, especially since, given the choice, many students would prefer to read **expository** over **narrative** text.[2] At the end of this chapter, the section titled "Integrative Readers" describes presents a number of strategies for teaching text structure to adults.

THE READER'S STANCE

When a student has difficulty retaining information from a text, a red flag is raised, and educators might discern that the student has a comprehension "problem." However, we need to consider that the extent to which a reader retains information from a text partially depends on the reader's stance. After you've read a newspaper, what type of information do you retain? Do you find that it is easier to remember a story from the headline news or the results of a sports match than it is to remember your personal horoscope? Consider the last novel you read that you just couldn't put down. What do you remember about this reading experience: the author's name, the characters' names, the setting, the plot, or perhaps just the title? Perhaps you simply recall the feeling you had when you finished reading.

Rosenblatt (1978, 1985), an American educator, developed a reader-response theory that helps to explain the reader's stance. Reader response refers to the transaction between the reader and the text. Rosenblatt has argued that readers adopt different stances or approaches towards text, depending on the nature of the text and their purpose for reading it. The reader's stance falls along a reader-response continuum, ranging from **aesthetic** to **efferent** reading. In the efferent stance, the reader's attention is focused on information to be taken away from the text. In the aesthetic stance, the reader's attention is on the "lived-through experience of the text" and the thoughts, feelings, images, and associations evoked as the story is read. This response is concerned with the personal nature of the reading experience, rather than retention of information.

Some texts, such as literature, are more appropriate for aesthetic reading while an efferent stance is usually more appropriate for texts such as newspapers, textbooks, and reference materials. While reading text, the reader may alternate between the two stances, in some instances taking information away from a predominantly aesthetic reading, and in others enjoying and appreciating the aesthetic qualities of a predominantly efferent reading (Cox, 1992).

Rosenblatt believes that "most teaching leads students to adopt an efferent stance" as educators present reading tasks in a manner that move students away from their personal responses to the text (as cited in Zarrillo & Cox, 1992, p. 236). When students are taught that reading is principally for gathering information or efferent reading, they may question the value of their literacy practices in settings outside the classroom. How frequently do students read a passage and answer questions in the home, work, or community settings? In order for a match to occur between classroom activity and daily literacy activities, students need to participate in aesthetic *and* efferent reading in the classroom or tutorial situation.

The Text

While the reader's background knowledge, reading strategies, and stance play key roles in how he or she constructs meaning, meaning construction is also affected by the structure and language of the text itself. It is self-evident that the more "reader-friendly" a text is, the easier it will be for readers to access and comprehend the writer's intended meaning. The following section discusses the role that text structures and language choices play in helping readers to construct meaning. It begins with a brief description of the characteristics that make a text "considerate," a term coined by Armbruster (1984). The next section provides an overview of the plain language movement.

CONSIDERATE TEXT

Considerate text contains particular features such as coherence, control of concept density, and the use of organizational signals and instructional devices. According to a group of American researchers, "coherence is the extent to which the sequencing of ideas in a text makes sense and the extent to which the language used to present those ideas makes the nature of the ideas and their relationships apparent" (McKeown, Beck, Sinatra, & Loxterman, 1992, p. 79). In a nutshell, coherence refers to a clear, logical text structure that flows easily from one idea to the next. The concept of coherence plays an important role in comprehension; and according to some, it is the text factor that exerts the strongest influence on comprehension and learning (Armbruster, 1984). Coherence is affected by the overall organization of the information in the text and by cohesive devices that provide links between sentences (see Figure 5.9).

Density of concepts refers to the rate at which new ideas and vocabulary are introduced. Sometimes, you will find that expository or non-fiction texts introduce a lot of new ideas and vocabulary without giving a sufficient number of

Figure 5.9 • Cohesive Devices

Cohesive Devices	Explanation	Example
Reference	A word that cannot be understood in its own right. It makes reference to something else for its interpretation. Pronouns, adverbs, and adjectives are common references.	*Terry* found a stray *cat*. *He* gave *it* some milk.
Synonym	Using words with similar meanings	praise, tribute, accolade
Connective	Linking two ideas so that the understanding of the second idea is related to the understanding of the first idea	"therefore," "because," "but," "then"

SOURCE: Adapted from Lipson, M.Y. & Wixson, K.K. (1991). *Assessment & instruction of reading disability: An interactive approach.* New York, NY: Harper Collins.

examples. This will probably cause a reader to become overloaded and result in poor comprehension. Ideally, text should introduce an idea, clarify it, and then provide examples.

Organizational signals are devices that emphasize the topics of a text and their organization. Well-organized texts are highlighted by signals such as titles, overviews, headings, topic sentences, and summaries. Instructional devices help the reader to understand the text's purpose, organization, and content. Such devices include a table of contents, a glossary, an index, and diagrams.

THE PLAIN LANGUAGE MOVEMENT

Advocates for plain language and considerate text have much in common. Both contend that the use of language and language structures that are clear and direct make public texts and documents more accessible. There are, however, two major differences between the two:

- The plain language movement uses a collaborative, reader-centred *process* during the development of the document, whereas considerate text is a *product* produced with the reader in mind, but without direct involvement of the reading audience.

- Plain language is part of a global, political movement, whereas "considerate text" is an apolitical term commonly used by reading specialists.

In today's society, individuals need access to information on political, social, and/or economic issues that affect their lives, as well as on issues that affect them personally, such as access to health services (Campbell, 1993). Although all citizens have an equal right to information and opportunities, many people are denied this right as written documents and public education materials are usually not written in plain language. Steinberg (1991) defines plain language as "language that reflects the interests and needs of the reader and consumer rather than the legal, bureaucratic, or technological interests of the writer or of the organization that the writer represents" (p. 7). Consumers, for example, are continually being asked to sign on the dotted line for insurance, loan, and rental agreements; vehicle purchase contracts; mortgages; warranties; and memberships. Think back to the last time you signed a contract or letter of agreement. Did you read the fine print? How did you feel when you saw the fine print? If consumers with well-developed literacy skills feel frustrated trying to understand the fine print, what emotions would an adult with low-literacy skills experience?

> ▶ Although all citizens have an equal right to information and opportunities, many people are denied this right as written documents and public education materials are usually not written in plain language.

The goal of the plain language movement is to advocate and promote communication that enables people to understand information that is important to their lives (Bowen, Duffy & Steinberg, 1986). To achieve this goal, a three-step process, described in *Plain Language Clear and Simple–Trainer's Guide* (1994) is recommended (see Figure 5.8). The first step in the process, audience analysis, is understanding the needs of the audience who will be reading the document. In the second step, writing, revising, and designing, the readers' needs must be considered along with the needs of the organization that is producing the document. The final step, piloting, involves testing the document with the intended audience to make sure it is effective and meets the needs of all parties. After testing, the document is revised according to the feedback received from the intended audience.

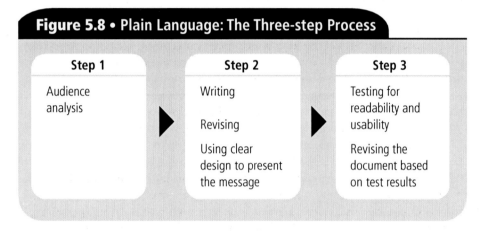

Figure 5.8 • Plain Language: The Three-step Process

Step 1
Audience analysis

Step 2
Writing

Revising

Using clear design to present the message

Step 3
Testing for readability and usability

Revising the document based on test results

SOURCE: Information Management and Economics. (1994). *Plain language: Clear and simple – trainer's guide*. Ottawa, ON: Canada Communication Group Publishing.

The plain language movement has had its the greatest influence on the development of legislation to regulate the clarity of consumer contracts. Plain language laws have been developed in Canada and the United States to ensure that the consumer is on an equal footing with the private and public sectors when signing documents. On July 5, 1990, the Alberta Legislature passed the *Financial Consumers Act*. This act, which became the first piece of plain language legislation to be adopted in Canada, states that certain consumer documents must be written in clear and understandable language. In the United States, the first plain language law—the *Sullivan Act*—was passed in New York in 1978. This law required certain consumer contracts for personal, household, and family purposes to be written in a clear and coherent manner. By 1994, 30 states had passed legislation to control the readability of rental agreements, and 10 states had passed legislation that requires plain language in consumer contracts (Information Management and Economics, 1994).

The plain language movement has provided opportunities for adult literacy educators to make changes in the area of access to information. The collaborative efforts of literacy organizations, provincial governments, hospitals, health clinics, legal advocacy groups, labor unions, and community organizations have resulted in a wide array of documents written in plain language. Health centres and organizations, for example, provide written information that uses plain language to describe medical conditions and treatments. Social assistance and other income security programs are making guides that outline services and benefits, and the rights and responsibilities of recipients. Clearly, great strides have been made in advocacy efforts to promote plain language. These efforts need to be maintained or there is the danger that the plain language movement, like other movements, will falter and fade due to a lack of political will.

Like all movements, plain language is not without its critics. A popular criticism is that simplifying the language or "dumbing it down" results in documents that do not include important nuances or "shades of grey." Plain language advocates rally against this criticism by responding that plain language doesn't mean simplistic, but rather clear and precise. The U.S. Securities and Exchange Commission explains that plain language "…does not mean deleting complex information to make the document easier to understand. Using plain English assures the orderly and clear presentation of complex information so that investors have the best possible chance of understanding it" (as cited in Mazur, 2000, p. 207). Both proponents have valid points, but they need to acknowledge that the inclusion or exclusion of nuances is not a function of plain language, rather, it is dependent on the expertise of the writer.

In many respects, the immediate lessons for adult literacy educators are clear. As was pointed out previously, many struggling adult readers tend to blame themselves for their inability to read. It would be fruitful for educators to point out to these readers that sometimes the fault may lie with the text, not with them. Documents, forms, articles, and directions that are obtuse or jargon-filled present a difficult reading task for even the most proficient reader. This does not mean that such texts should not be part of an adult reading program. Not only do they represent a reality in students' lives—somehow adults need strategies for reading such texts—they can also provide the stimulation for group analysis and critique.

Context

To fully appreciate the role that context plays in the construction of meaning, think of a text that has been interpreted in multiple ways throughout history. For example, religious texts, such as the Bible and the Qur'an have been subjected to multiple interpretations. It is apparent that the scriptures would be interpreted quite differently by fundamentalist preachers, United Church ministers, or Darwinian scholars. Similarly, the Qur'an would be interpreted from a different perspective by feminists, Muslims, or deep fundamentalists like the Taliban. The preceding examples illustrate how the construction of meaning is dependent on who is interpreting the text; when, where, and why it is being interpreted; and what the interpretation is going to be used for. In essence, every act of meaning construction is socially, culturally, and politically situated and contextualized. Some of these contextual factors are discussed below.

LITERACY GOALS AND STRATEGIES

Fluent readers modify their reading strategies according to their reading goal or purpose. As you sort through supermarket flyers, you might scan the headings for household items that you need. When you check your e-mails, you scan the list to locate the ones you need to respond to immediately. When you read a schedule, you probably skim it to locate specific information such as times and locations. If you're studying for a test, you might formulate questions and recite the answers in your head. If you're reading a mystery novel, you might read the last page to satisfy your curiosity.

The construction of meaning will be affected by a reader's purpose and the reading strategies he/she employs. Sometimes, adult literacy students need to be taught the importance of formulating a reading goal and choosing an appropriate strategy to meet that goal. The chart in Figure 5.10 can be used to heighten students' awareness of how they read each piece of text differently, depending upon their purpose(s). Begin by asking the students to share some of the reading they have engaged in during the past week. Then, ask them to consider **why** they read the material and **how** they read it.

Figure 5.10

Reading Material	Why I Read It	How I Read It
TV Guide	To look for a movie	Skim
Supermarket flyer	Check sale items	Scan
Child's report card	Assurance that child is progressing	Slowly

LITERACY PRACTICES, EVENTS, AND DOMAINS

> The notion of *literacy practices* offers a powerful way of conceptualizing the link between the activities of reading and writing and the social structures in which they are embedded and which they help shape... In the simplest sense literacy practices are what people do with literacy. (Barton & Hamilton, 2000, p. 7)

Barton and Hamilton (2000) introduce a social theory of literacy that incorporates literacy practices, events, and domains. The term "literacy practices" refers to the functions of text and **what** it is being used for. In order to answer the question "What do people do with literacy?" one often needs to dig beneath the surface. At the surface level, people have literacy goals or purposes such as reading to locate information, and reading for pleasure. At a deeper level, people engage in literacy practices for economic gain, for socio-political change, for civil rights, for spirituality, for power, for education, for liberation, and for status (Brandt, 1999).

Although it is difficult to observe a literacy practice because practices involve values, attitudes, emotions, and social relationships, it is possible to observe literacy events. A literacy event is an activity that usually involves written text and spoken language (Barton & Hamilton, 2000). Literacy events are situated in different domains, such as the home, the school, the workplace, and the community. These events fall within the broader realm of literacy practices, and both relate to broader social structures and cultural practices. In order to understand this relationship, let's use a common literacy event—reading a novel.

In the home, the reading of a novel can be used to resist cultural domination. During the reign of the Taliban in Afghanistan during the 1990s, housewives secretly read books as a means of asserting their right to their own pleasurable activity in a patriarchical society. In the workplace, employees might read a novel during work hours as a means of resisting inequitable power relationships between the employer and employees. In these two examples, the readers would probably be engaged in aesthetic reading, where their major concern is the personal nature of the reading experience. In the school, the reading of a novel supports dominant literacy practices in which one must study and retain information, in order to receive a good mark. In this example, the readers' major concern, though not choice, might be the retention of information. Clearly, when one reads a novel, the construction of meaning will be affected by the literacy event, the literacy practice, and the domain.

Comprehension Patterns

THE EXTENT TO WHICH students use text information and background knowledge to construct meaning from what they read is a pivotal factor in their ability to comprehend what they read. Students' answers to well-designed **factual** and **inferential** comprehension questions can help you to determine the extent to which students rely on text information and background knowledge. Determining how students interact with text can assist in identifying the students' comprehension patterns and subsequently help develop a responsive instructional program.

Text-based Readers

Students with a text-based comprehension pattern are usually able to answer factual comprehension questions posed by the teacher as part of a workbook response activity. By definition, the answers to these types of questions are found in the text or passage. By default, text-based students have difficulty answering inference questions, which require that they use background knowledge and text information to "read between the lines."

> Since many adults may not have been exposed to explicit comprehension instruction, it is important that they receive this instruction in their adult upgrading classes or tutorials. If you think back to your school days, can you recall being taught *how* to comprehend text? During Grades 1 and 2, I read the *Dick and Jane* readers. After reading each story, the teacher would ask the class a set of comprehension questions. During Grade 3, we used the *Uncle Funny Bunny* series, which consisted of a textbook and a set of workbooks. Again, we weren't taught *how* to comprehend text; rather, we completed workbook activities that *tested* our comprehension.

In addition, text-based readers tend not to use their background knowledge to make predictions about events that are going to unfold in the next sentence, paragraph, or page. What follows are three possible explanations for this type of reading behaviour.

In the first place, text-based readers may not realize that they "must assert power to have meaningful transactions with texts" (Smith, 1992, p. 144). Smith conducted a study of the interpretive processes of ten Grade 9 students, half of whom were reading below grade level, and half of whom were reading above grade level as they read two stories. He distinguished between "submission" — the reader's passive acceptance of the text as the repository of meaning—and "surrender"—the reader's willingness to enter the world of the story and create meaning. Smith found that the less successful readers submitted to the text's authority rather than exercising an active role in shaping textual meaning. Although this study was conducted with adolescents, it raises many questions about the ways in which adult literacy students engage with text.

Often, as a result of their experiences with formal reading instruction, adult students are hesitant to "read between the lines," preferring instead to "stick to the facts." When asked an inferential question, students sometimes respond with the phrase "It didn't say." Is it possible that this type of response suggests the submission mode and a reluctance to exert power over the text? I believe that a productive first step to becoming an active reader is understanding the importance of asserting control and accepting that one can exert power over text. Conversations with students about "reading the lines" and "reading *between* the lines" help educators to understand the degree of power that student readers assert in their reading.

Second, if students are not familiar with the topic of a passage, they will not possess the necessary background knowledge to make inferences *and* predictions. As a teacher in rural Nigeria, I witnessed how difficult it was for students to make inferences and predictions about topics that were foreign to their experiences. The Nigerian school system used the British curriculum, which meant that the students and I were subjected to books such as *The Kon-Tiki Expedition*. Together, the students and I struggled in our efforts to construct meaning from the British literature that contained unfamiliar subject matter, ideology, concepts, and language.

Third, students with a text-based reading comprehension pattern may have a great deal of experience in answering factual questions, but limited experience in answering inferential questions. A study conducted by three American researchers to examine classroom dynamics in 20 adult literacy classrooms supports this hypothesis. These classrooms were situated in seven states and were chosen to maximize program and learner diversity. The findings indicated that even though these educators expressed the intention of being learner-centred, a sequence of questioning and answering designed to elicit correct, factual answers was the predominant activity in each classroom (Beder, Medina & Eberly, 2000; Beder, 2001). If students are continually exposed to this type of instruction, they are receiving a subliminal message that as readers they should adopt a passive role.

Post-reading questions provide the educator with insights into how students interact with text as they read. Students with a text-based pattern, as indicated by their responses to questions, can benefit from being taught strategies that

▶ **When asked an inferential question, students sometimes respond with the phrase "It didn't say." Is it possible that this type of response suggests the submission mode and a reluctance to exert power over the text?**

enable them to activate their background knowledge to make inferences. The next section describes two strategies designed to help students relate their background knowledge to text information in order to broaden and deepen the meanings they construct.

Directed-reading thinking activity (DRTA)

For the past three decades, educators have used the DRTA to develop students' ability to read critically and reflectively. This strategy was developed by Stauffer (1969), who believed that reading is a thinking process that involves the reader in using his/her own experiences to reconstruct the author's ideas. The DRTA encourages readers to use their background knowledge to predict what might happen in a story and to use cues from the text to evaluate and revise these predictions. This strategy consists of five steps outlined below:

1 Select a narrative passage that provides opportunities for prediction. The length of the passage should be suitable for a 15-to-20 minute lesson. Prior to the lesson, identify several "natural" pause points in the text where the students can pause to make a prediction. Figure 5.11 on the following page uses checkmarks to illustrate possible points in the text where the students could pause to make a prediction.

2 Encourage students to make an initial prediction based on the title of the story or the first paragraph. Predictions can be elicited by posing questions such as these:

- *What do you think this story will be about?*
- *What do you think will happen in the story?*
- *Why do you think so?*

Bainbridge and Malicky (2000) stress the importance of the last question, because it provides an opportunity for students to utilize their background knowledge and the cues in the title or first paragraph. It also invites supported prediction rather than wild "guessing"—students need to be aware that they need some accountability to the text. The students' predictions can be listed on the blackboard or flipchart paper.

3 Ask the students to read silently to a certain point in the text to determine if their initial prediction(s) were confirmed or disproved. Then ask the students for evidence from the story that supports the confirmed prediction. The students can discuss the text information that verifies or disproves their predictions.

4 Repeat the process of predicting, reading, and evaluating for the subsequent pieces of text. Continue using this process until the entire passage has been read.

Figure 5.11 • Pause Points for DRTA

The Big Goof ✔

Jan is in love. She is in love with Bill. Bill lives next door. Bill does not love Jan. But Jan has a plan. ✔ She makes pies for Bill. But Bill does not care. She cuts his grass. But Bill does not care. She washes his car. But Bill does not care. Or does he? One day, Jan gets a call. It is Bill. ✔ "Let's go for coffee," Bill said. "Okay," said Jan. "Yes!" Jan does her hair. She puts on her make-up. She puts on her best dress. Jan is ready. Jan and Bill go to a donut shop. Bill talks about his job. He talks for hours. And hours. And hours. He talks and talks on his cell. He says mean things to the waitress. ✔ Jan goes home. Jan does not talk to Bill. She does not answer the door. She does not answer the phone. Jan is happy. But Bill is a big goof.

SOURCE: Kita-Bradley, L. (2000). *The big goof*. Edmonton, AB: Grass Roots Press.

Invisible messages technique

The purpose of this strategy is to show students how to use background knowledge and text cues to make inferences. To begin the lesson, discuss the connection between making inferences and understanding the text. Next, demonstrate how to make an inference by using the think-aloud process that was described earlier in this chapter. Then, ask the students to read a short portion of text and to look for "invisible messages" or information that has not been explicitly stated by the author. After the students have generated some inferences, ask them to validate their invisible messages with text cues and their background knowledge.

Biographies are a good source of text for making inferences. Students can make inferences about a person's character by reading about their actions. Figure 5.12 on page 114 is an example of a character sketch chart about Mary Ann Shadd, an Afro-American who was born in 1823.

Johnson and Johnson (1986) identified ten different types of inferences (see Figure 5.13 on page 114). The text cues in the character sketch chart provide examples of inferences drawn from actions. When you teach readers to use inferences, it might be helpful to discuss the different types of inferences and to provide examples.

Figure 5.12 • Character Sketch Chart

Text cues	Invisible Message
She set up a private school for escaped slaves.	She believed in education. She was brave and determined. She was a visionary.
As a lawyer, she gave her services to the poor for free.	She was intelligent and kind.
She started a newspaper to let others know about the anti-slavery movement and to give a voice to black people in Canada.	She believed in democracy. She was articulate.

Figure 5.13 • Types of Inferences

Type of Inference	Example
Location	One Sunday morning, the pastor asked me to read some verses from the Bible. (Where was she?)
Time	The leaves were starting to turn colour. (What is the season?)
Action	She set up a private school for escaped slaves. (What did she believe in?)
Instrument	Once it became hot, she began to curl her hair. (What tool or device did she use?)
Object	The majestic peaks were obscured by the clouds. (What were the majestic peaks?)
Category	I have about 900 cards, Pro Set and Score Brands. (What type of cards are these?)
Occupation or Pastime	I had to clean the ice, check the air compressor and wash the floor. (What was this person's occupation?)
Cause-Effect	The roads were blocked and no trains were running, so Dad had to plow a road across the field to the highway. (What caused this situation?)
Problem-Solution	She was getting too old to take care of herself. (What should she do about this problem?)
Feeling-Attitude	When I received my degree, tears came to my father's eyes. (What emotion was the father experiencing?)

SOURCE: Johnson, D.D. & Johnson, B. (1986). Highlighting vocabulary in inferential vocabulary instruction. *Journal of Reading, 29*(7), 622-625.

Knowledge-based Readers

Some readers tend to embellish stories with little or no concern for or accountability to the text information. When they retell a story, they often go off on a tangent about how a similar experience happened to them, or they begin to make up a story that has only a fleeting resemblance to the text original except for the use of an occasional word or phrase. The term "knowledge-based" describes a reader with this type of comprehension pattern.

Students with a knowledge-based comprehension pattern use their background knowledge, rather than information from the text, when they answer comprehension questions. They have more success with answering inference questions than factual questions. Although it is appropriate to use background knowledge, an over-reliance on prior knowledge can lead to problems as the reader's understanding of the passage may differ from the author's intended meaning.

In order to extend their abilities to read more in-depth, knowledge-based readers need to develop strategies that enable them to attend more closely to the text information as they read. While reading narrative passages, they need to pay more attention to the characters, the setting, the plot, and the themes. When they are reading expository passages, they need to pay more attention to the main idea and details so that they can remember and retain text information. The next section describes two strategies designed to help students relate the text information to their background knowledge.

Herringbone technique

This strategy is aimed at directing students' attention to specific key details in the text. As you introduce this strategy, explain the importance of paying attention to the information on the page. Then show the student the Herringbone form and demonstrate how to record information by "walking through" the strategy (see Figure 5.14 on page 116). The Herringbone form provides a structure that assists students in attending to and remembering the text information.

Begin by selecting a piece of text for the students to read. Newspaper stories work well as they are usually structured around the five "w" questions. As the students read the selection, encourage them to ask six basic comprehension questions:

Who is involved?   **Where** was it done?
What did this person or group do?   **When** did they do it?
Why did it happen?   **How** was it accomplished?

During or after reading the selection, the student can record the answers to these questions in the Herringbone outline. As an alternative to the Herringbone outline, the students can use a question grid to analyze the information in a sentence or paragraph (see Figure 5.15 on page 116). You can vary the number or order of the question words in the grid. It all depends on the details you want the student to locate. The first grid, with the questions Who? What? When? Where? and Why? is completed.

Figure 5.14 • Recording Text Information in a Herringbone Form

TEXT:

Gold was found in British Columbia in the 1850s and 1860s. News of the gold spread fast. Many people wanted to get rich. They travelled a long way to search for gold. People came from the States, Europe, and China.

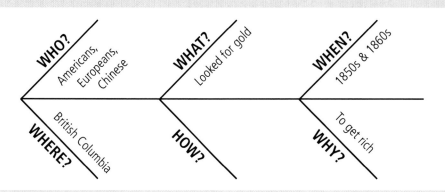

SOURCE: Tierney, R.J., Readence, J.E., Dishner, E.K. (1990). *Reading strategies and practices: A compendium.* Toronto, ON: Allyn and Bacon.

Figure 5.15 • Question Grids

Who?	What?	When?	Where?	Why?
People from the States, Europe, and China.	Looked for gold	1850s & 1860s	B.C.	To get rich

Where?		Who?		What?	

When?	Who?	What?	Where?

SOURCE: Davey, B. (1983). Think aloud–Modelling the cognitive processes of reading comprehension. *Journal of Reading 27*(1), p.46.

The ReQuest procedure

This strategy, which was developed by Manzo (1969) has been used by educators for the past three decades. The procedure is designed to encourage students to formulate their own questions about the material they are reading, in order to attend to and process text more carefully. Throughout the procedure, it is important to ask clear, concise questions and to reinforce similar behaviour in the student through positive feedback. This is an effective strategy for knowledge-based readers who need to pay more attention to the text information.

The ReQuest Procedure, which works best in a one-to-one instructional setting, consists of the following steps:

1 Select a paragraph that is at the student's instructional reading level. Both you and the student should have a copy of the paragraph.

2 You and the student read the first sentence silently. Then the student asks you as many questions as he/she wants about that sentence.

3 You answer the questions, and if necessary, ask for unclear questions to be rephrased.

4 After all of the student's questions are answered, you and the student exchange roles. Both of you read the next sentence, and this time you question the student, asking different questions that require the student to synthesize information from two or more sentences. Periodically, you should require the student to verify his/her responses by reference to the text.

5 The procedure should continue for approximately 15 to 20 minutes or until the paragraph has been read.

Figure 5.16 on page 118 provides an example of dialogue between a tutor and a student using the ReQuest Procedure. The text came from a local community newspaper. The ReQuest Procedure can also be used in a classroom setting. The students can try to "stump" the educator by asking difficult questions.

Figure 5.16 • Request Procedure Dialogue

Dialogue	Text	Comments
Tutor: Let's read the first sentence silently. Then, we can take turns asking questions about the sentence. Let's start by having you ask me a question.	Two men have been charged after one of them tried to escape from custody in Kamloops last week.	
Student: Okay, how many men were charged?		
Tutor: Two. Okay, my turn. Where were they?		
Student: In jail in Kamloops.		
Tutor: Good. Do you want to try asking me another question?		
Student: Um, what did they do to get into the newspaper?		
Tutor: Do you mean what did they do that caused a reporter to write an article about them?		The tutor is not sure about what the student is asking; so the tutor asks for clarification.
Student: Yeah.		
Tutor: Well, one of them tried to escape. The other might have been helping, but it didn't say.		
Student: Okay, that's all.		
Tutor: Let's read the next sentence, and then I'll ask a question.	On December 12, a warden at the jail heard a loud noise and found Shawn Bradley banging on the bars of his cell, while farther down the row, Bill Smith was trying to remove a ceiling vent.	
Tutor: Why was Shawn banging on the bars?		The tutor asks a question that requires the student to combine information from the two sentences.
Student: He wanted to make a noise so that Bill could escape. Here's one for you. How was Bill planning to escape?		
Tutor: He was going to go up in the vent. I guess he was a small guy. I don't think I'd fit up in a vent.		The tutor answers the question and makes an inference statement.

Integrative Readers

Students with an integrative comprehension pattern use a combination of background knowledge and text information in an effort to understand the author's message. Students who demonstrate this pattern benefit from instructional strategies before, during, and after reading that focus on combining the use of knowledge and text to construct meaning. This type of reader is actively involved with the text and uses his/her background knowledge to make inferences and predictions, and to answer inference questions. This type of reader also understands the importance of paying attention to the author's message and has the ability to answer factual questions correctly.

Many adult basic education programs require students to complete courses in English, math, science, and social studies, which means that a major focus for students is on learning from expository texts. Although students with an integrative comprehension pattern are effective readers in some situations, awareness and instruction in **expository text structures** will benefit their overall reading and writing abilities. The five most common types of organizational patterns for expository material are generalization, cause-effect, comparison-contrast, sequence, and enumeration (Campbell & Brokop, 1998).

Text structure instruction

Expository text structure instruction integrates reading and writing activities. The following steps can be followed to teach text structure to adults.

❶ Discuss the role that text structure plays in enabling or supporting active comprehension. The analogy of shopping in a grocery store can be used to explain the importance of knowing organizational patterns.

❷ Use a real-life example to explain text structure. If you're introducing enumeration, for instance, ask the student to describe a favourite person in his/her life. Then, explain how this structure is used by authors to provide information about a topic, person, place, or thing. The author organizes the information by listing features, characteristics, and examples. You might want to mention that signal and phrases such as "some," "several," "other," "many," "also," "too," and "for example" clue the reader into this structure.

❸ Provide a short passage that illustrates the text structure (see Figure 5.17 on page 120).

❹ Present the student with a frame or graphic organizer that can be used to diagram the text structure (see Figure 5.18 on page 120). Graphic organizers illustrate the key parts of a whole and their relations, providing a holistic, visual framework that words alone cannot convey. Tarasoff (2000) compiled a set of graphic organizers that can be used for individual and classroom instruction.

5 Use the graphic organizer to write a summary of the passage. As a follow-up activity, a graphic organizer can be developed as a basis for writing a short passage or produce a piece of writing on another topic.

Figure 5.17 • Enumeration Passage

Premenstrual Syndrome

As many as eight out of ten women have physical and emotional symptoms of premenstrual syndrome, or PMS. While the symptoms can be uncomfortable and upsetting, PMS can be easily managed in many cases. A healthy diet and self-care can result in more comfort and less stress, every month.

You may have PMS if you have these physical symptoms up to two weeks before your period: exhaustion; sleep disturbances; breast swelling; bloating; weight gain; acne; cravings for sweets; constipation, then diarrhea. The emotional symptoms can be even more difficult to deal with than the physical. Common emotional symptoms include irritability; depression; anxiety; confusion; feeling out of control. For some women, these symptoms are mild. For others, symptoms are severe and make life very difficult. While there are many theories about the cause of PMS, scientists agree that it's real, and not "all in your head."

Figure 5.18 • Graphical Organizer

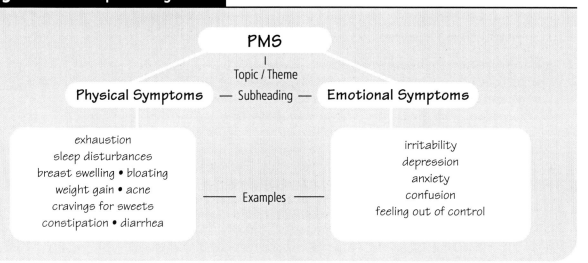

Students with an integrative comprehension pattern might also require instruction in study skills in order to retain the content of expository text. Some integrative readers are able to acquire study skills independently. Others need explicit instruction in this area. In order to assess students' study skills, ask them what they do to prepare for a test. You may find that many integrative readers study by simply rereading the text. The SQ3R, which is described on the following page is a systematic approach to reading and studying expository text.

SQ3R

SQ3R is one of the oldest and most popular study methods (Robinson, 1946). The steps involved in SQ3R are described below.

> Step 1: <u>S</u>urvey

The student previews a chapter of a book or a section of an expository text by quickly reading the title, headings, and beginning and concluding paragraphs. The student can also examine illustrations and diagrams. The survey, which takes approximately five to fifteen minutes, is intended to provide the students with an overview of the chapter content.

> Step 2: <u>Q</u>uestion

Next, the student turns the first heading into a question. If the heading in a science textbook is "Cloud Formation," the question might be "How do clouds form?" This activity serves to activate the student's background knowledge and helps set a purpose for reading.

> Step 3: <u>R</u>ead

This step, which is the first of the three "R" steps, requires an active search for the answer to the question posed in Step 2.

> Step 4: <u>R</u>ecite

Next, the student closes the book or passage and recite the answer to his/her question out loud. The student is encouraged to answer the question in his/her own words; in some cases, a visual learner might be more comfortable writing down the answer. Recitation helps the reader to monitor whether or not he/she has comprehended the material. In addition, recitation helps to fix the ideas in memory. After the student has recited the answer, Steps 2 - 4 are repeated for the rest of the chapter or selection.

> Step 5: <u>R</u>eview

After the student has completed reading the chapter, he/she spends about five minutes reading over notes. The student then covers up the notes and recalls the main points for each heading. The student can either recite the main points or write them out. He/she can also read each main heading and try to recall the supporting or explanatory information.

CHAPTER SUMMARY

Viewed from a social constructivist perspective, comprehension is a process whereby a reader constructs meaning by relating information and ideas in a text to his or her background knowledge within a social context. In essence, comprehension is a product of the interaction between text and reader. A reader's ability to comprehend is affected or influenced by two major factors: the reader and his or her view of how reading takes place, and the nature of the text and how it is written.

Because of their previous formal reading experiences, many readers view reading as a process whereby information is transmitted from the author to them. The emphasis for the reader is to remember all of the information in the text. Such readers are considered "text-based," and a number of teaching strategies designed to develop their ability to draw inferences or read beyond the text information are presented.

In contrast to "text-based" readers, "knowledge-based" readers tend to rely primarily on their background knowledge in order to comprehend what they read. Such readers benefit from instructional strategies that show them how to pay closer attention to the text and what the author is attempting to communicate. Several strategies have been developed to help readers pay closer attention to text. The goal of strategic comprehension instruction is to develop integrative readers who are able to balance their personal meaning constructions with a reasonable accountability to the text and the author's intended purpose.

Some adults might not be aware of how their thinking before, during, and after reading affects their comprehension. The ability to reflect on thinking is known as metacognitive awareness, and educators can help students to develop their awareness by sharing their own thinking during reading and by pointing out the types of thinking that proficient readers use as they read. Strategies designed to help readers develop metacognitive awareness were outlined.

The second major consideration in comprehension is the nature of the text to be read. Texts may be considered "considerate" when they are cohesive; and when they control concept density and use organizational signals and devices that provide explicit support for the reader's efforts to comprehend. In addition, when texts and documents are written in plain language, they reflect the interests and needs of the reader rather than those of the writer or issuing authority.

When texts are considerate and written in plain language, it is obvious that they are more readily accessible for adults with low-literacy skills. In the course of their daily lives, these same adults may encounter and be required to read conceptually dense, jargon-filled, and poorly written documents. Thus, a productive element of an adult literacy program may be helping students to critique such documents and texts in order to develop strategies for responding to them.

The importance of such a critique and response is important as it invites educators to come to terms with issues like accessibility and active participation. The next chapter expands the notion of balance in literacy instruction by placing reading instruction in a participatory context. ❖

References

Anderson, R.C. & Pearson, P.D. (1984). A schema-theoretic view of basic processes in reading comprehension. In P.D. Pearson (Ed.), *Handbook of reading research* (pp. 255-291). New York: Longman.

Armbruster, B.B. (1984). The problem of "inconsiderate text." In G.G. Duffy, L.R. Roehler, & J. Mason (Eds.), *Comprehension instruction* (pp. 202-217). New York: Longman.

Atwood, M. (1985). *The handmaid's tale.* Toronto, ON: McClelland and Stewart.

Bainbridge, J. & Malicky, G. (2000). *Constructing meaning: Balancing elementary language arts* (2nd ed.). Toronto, ON: Harcourt Canada.

Barton, D. & Hamilton, M. (2000). Literacy practices. In D. Barton, M. Hamilton, & R. Ivanic (Eds.), *Situated literacies: Reading and writing in context* (pp. 7-15). New York: Routledge.

Beder, H. (2001). *Teaching in adult literacy education: Learner-centred intentions, teacher-directed instruction.* Paper presented at the American Education Research Conference.

Beder, H., Medina, P. & Eberly, M. (2000). *The adult literacy classroom as a social system.* Paper presented at the American Education Research Conference.

Becker, R.R. (1999). Reader response: Students develop text understanding. *Reading Horizons, 40*(2), 103-126.

Bowen, B.A. Duffy, B.A. & Steinberg, E.R. (1986). *Analyzing the various approaches of plain language laws* (CDC Tech. Rep. No. 29). Pittsburgh, PA: Communications Design Centre, Carnegie-Mellon University.

Brandt, D. (1999). Literacy learning and economic change. *Harvard Educational Review, 69*(4), 373-394.

Campbell, P. (1993). About literacy in Canada. In P. Faid (Ed.), *Working for literacy: Public attitudes and political persuasion* (pp. 26-54). Calgary, AB: Alberta Association for Adult Literacy.

Campbell, P. & Brokop, F. (1998). *Supplemental training for practitioners in literacy Education* (STAPLE). Calgary, AB: Literacy Coordinators of Alberta. Distributed by Grass Roots Press.

Cox, S.T. (1992). Perspectives on stance in response to literature: A theoretical and historical framework. In J. Many & C. Cox (Eds.), *Reader stance & literary understanding: Exploring the theories, research, & practice* (pp. 11-22). Norwood, MJ: Ablex.

Crummey, M. (2001). *River thieves.* Toronto, ON: Doubleday Canada.

Cunningham, J.W. & Wall, L.K. (1994). Teaching good readers to comprehend better. *Journal of Reading, 37*(6), 480-486.

Davey, B. (1983). Think aloud–modelling the cognitive processes of reading comprehension. *Journal of Reading, 27*(1), 44-47.

Devine, T.G. (1986). *Teaching reading comprehension: From theory to practice.* Toronto, ON: Allyn and Bacon, Inc.

Enciso, P. (1992). Creating the story world. A case study of a young reader's engagement strategies and stances. In J. Many & C. Cox (Eds.), *Reader stance and literary understanding: Exploring the theories, research, & practice* (pp. 75-101). Norwood, NJ: Ablex.

Financial Consumers Act, Chapter F-9.5 Statutes of Alberta (1990).

Giroux, H. & Simon, R. (1989). Popular culture and critical pedagogy: Everyday life as a basis for curriculum knowledge. In H. Giroux & P. McLaren (Eds.), *Critical pedagogy, the state, and cultural struggle* (pp. 236-252). Albany, NY: State University of New York Press.

Information Management and Economics. (1994). Plain language: *Clear and simple – trainer's guide.* Ottawa, ON: Canada Communication Group Publishing.

Johnson, D.D. & Johnson, B. (1986). Highlighting vocabulary in inferential vocabulary instruction. *Journal of Reading, 29*(7), 622-625.

Jones, B.F., Pierce, J. & Hunter, B. (1988-1989). Teaching children to construct graphic representations. *Educational Leadership, 46,* 20-25.

Kita-Bradley, L. (2000). *The big goof.* Edmonton, AB: Grass Roots Press.

Lamb, W. (1992). *She's come undone.* New York: Simon and Schuster.

Lipson, M.Y. & Wixson, K.K. (1991). *Assessment & instruction of reading disability: An interactive approach.* New York: Harper Collins.

Manzo, A.V. (1969). The request procedure. *Journal of Reading, 13*(2), 123-126.

Mazur, B. (2000). Revisiting plain language. *Technical Communication, 47*(2), 205-211.

McCarthy M. and Carter R. (1994). *Language as discourse: Perspectives for language teaching.* London: Longman.

McKeown, M.G., Beck, I.L., Sinatra, G.M. & Loxterman, J.A. (1992). The contribution of prior knowledge and coherent text to comprehension. *Reading Research Quarterly, 27*(1), 79-93.

Ogle, D. (1986). K-W-L: A teaching model that develops active reading of expository text. *The Reading Teacher, 39*(6), 564-570.

Pappas, C.C. & Pettegrew, B.S. (1998). The role of genre in the psycholinguistic guessing game of reading. *Language Arts, 75*(1), 36-44.

Pearson, P.D. & Johnson, D.D. (1978). *Teaching reading comprehension.* New York: Holt, Rinehart, and Winston.

Pressley, M. (2000). What should comprehension instruction be the instruction of? In M.L. Kamil, P.B. Mosenthal, P.D. Pearson & R. Barr (Eds.), *Handbook of reading research: Volume III* (pp. 545-561). Mahwah, NJ: Lawrence Erlbaum Associates.

Pressley, M. & Afflerbach, A. (1995). *Verbal protocols of reading: The nature of constructively responsive reading.* Hillsdale, NJ: Lawrence Erlbaum Associates.

Robinson, F.P. (1946). *Effective study.* New York: Harper and Bros.

Rosenblatt, L. (1978). *The reader, the text, the poem: The transactional theory of the literary work.* Carbondale, IL: Southern Illinois University Press.

Rosenblatt, L. (1985). The transactional theory of the literary work: Implications for research. In C. Cooper (Ed.), *Researching response to literature and the teaching of literature: Points of departure* (pp. 35-53). Norwood, NJ: Ablex Publishing.

Rumelhart, D.E. (1977). *Introduction to human information processing theory.* New York: John Wiley & Sons.

Smith, M.W. (1992). Submission versus control in literary transactions. In J. Many & C. Cox (Eds.), *Reader stance & literary understanding: Exploring the theories, research, & practice* (pp. 143-161). Norwood, NJ: Ablex.

Stauffer, R.G. (1969). *Teaching reading as a thinking process.* New York: Harper & Row Publishers.

Steinberg, E. (Ed.). (1991). *Plain language: Principles and practice.* Detroit, MI: Wayne State University Press.

Tarasoff, M. (2000). *Reading instruction that makes sense: Black line masters.* Victoria, BC: Active Learning Institute.

Tierney, R.J., Readence, J.E., Dishner, E.K. (1990). *Reading strategies and practices: A compendium.* Toronto, ON: Allyn and Bacon.

Wilson, P.T. & Anderson, R.C. (1986). What they don't know will hurt them: The role of prior knowledge in comprehension. In J. Orasanu (Ed.), *Reading comprehension: From research to practice* (pp. 31-48). Hillsdale, NJ: Erlbaum.

Wolff, B. (2002, January 14). The aces on bridge. *Edmonton Journal,* p. C5.

Zarrillo, J. & Cox, C. (1992). Efferent and aesthetic teaching. In J. Many & C. Cox (Eds.), *Reader stance & literary understanding: Exploring the theories, research, & practice* (143-161). Norwood, NJ: Ablex.

Notes

1   Schemata is the plural of schema.

2   In 1998, Campbell and Brokop organized 24 focus groups in western, central, eastern, and northern Canada. In total, 201 Adult Basic Education (ABE) students participated. The purpose of these groups was to determine the reading interests of ABE students. The findings indicated that 84 percent of the students preferred reading expository text, while only 16 percent preferred reading narrative text.

CHAPTER SIX

Teaching Reading in a Participatory Context

Introduction

An educator's entry into participatory education often begins with a questioning of the status quo. My entry point occurred in the late 1980s, when I served on an advisory committee for *English Express*, a newspaper written in plain language for adult literacy students. The chair of the committee asked me to recruit a student representative to serve on the committee. I approached Julia, a confident and vocal student whose literacy abilities were quite well developed. Julia agreed to serve on the committee, only to resign after one year. During this year, Julia regularly attended meetings, but she was quiet and withdrawn, voicing her opinion(s) only when she was directly asked a question. Julia's silence prompted me to start thinking about the issues of representation and voice, and what I, as a literacy educator, was doing to contribute to Julia's silence.

In 1991, I chose participatory education as the focus of my doctoral work, and the substance of this work follows in this chapter. For those of you who are starting your career in adult education, it is my hope that some aspect of this chapter will serve as your entry point. For those colleagues already on this journey, I hope that this chapter will support and strengthen your commitment to participatory education.

The chapter opens with a summary of the origins of participatory education. This review is followed by a discussion of the three themes of participatory education:

- **Community:** Participatory education promotes the development of community by combining literacy education with social (inter)action.
- **Social Relations:** Participatory education examines and challenges inequitable power relations within hierarchical structures.

- **Knowledge:** Learning is built around the knowledge that students construct from their social, cultural, and political experiences.

The chapter ends with a description of the participatory curriculum. The participatory spiral and the problem-posing method are described; these are processes in which students share, create, analyze, and act on their knowledge and experiences. Throughout the chapter, the benefits and challenges of education are presented and discussed.

Participatory Education

Teaching reading in a participatory context creates opportunities for students to collectively read the word and the world around them. Ideally, participatory education is "a collective effort in which the participants are committed to building a just society through individual and socioeconomic transformation and ending domination through changing power relations" (Campbell, 2001, p. 1). This definition is a *vision* of how participatory education creates possibilities for moving beyond constructing meaning to bringing about change. This vision is the fuel that sustains educators who support participatory approaches in their programs and moves them forward when they encounter ideological and material barriers that prevent them from engaging in participatory practices. My practice and research have informed me that participatory education is a slow process in which students and educators take small steps toward making positive changes in their lives and their community. A positive change, for instance, occurs when students challenge inequitable power relations by taking a stand and speaking their minds.

Origins of Participatory Education[1]

The origins of participatory education can be traced to popular education, a model and approach to learning developed and pioneered by Brazilian educator Paulo Freire. Popular education has been used throughout Latin America and other Third World countries to promote literacy and to help people educate and organize themselves around issues such as health care, agricultural reform, elections, and working conditions. Participatory education and popular education are both based on socialist principles of equality and justice, with the goal of building a new, more humane, more democratic, and more just society. Both models involve a dialectical, collective process of sharing, analysis, and action. Popular education tends to be highly creative, relying on cultural forms (drama, drawing, music, stories, photos) as educational tools.

The major difference between popular education and participatory education is that they have evolved in different contexts. Popular education originated in Latin America, whereas participatory education has its roots in North America. Freire's work in literacy was rooted in developing countries, and the literacy campaigns he organized occurred in the context of revolutionary social change. The specific historical, political, cultural, social, and economic factors that fueled these literacy campaigns are different from those in the North American context. North American programs have incorporated and modified aspects of Freire's pedagogy, based on the recognition that social change is likely small-scale, rather than revolutionary as it may be in Third World countries.

The principles of participatory education have been applied in North American contexts since the early 20th century. In 1902, under the sponsorship of Frontier College in Ontario, educators worked in the labour camps alongside the labourers, seeking to establish educator-student relationships where all participants learned from each other (Cook, 1987; Krotz, Martin, & Fernandez, 1999). The Antigonish Movement in the later 1920s and early 1930s in Nova Scotia advocated a nonformal approach to education for economic development. In 1932, Myles Horton (Horton & Freire, 1990; Horton, Kohl, & Kohl, 1990) founded the Highlander Center in Tennessee, an adult educational center dedicated to helping people address and solve socioeconomic and political problems by mining their own experience and awareness. The Highlander Center has been integral to major social movements such as labour organizing in the 1930s and 1940s, the civil rights movement in the 1950s and 1960s, and environmental activism in the 1970s and 1980s. It is of more than passing interest to note that Rosa Parks, the black woman whose action sparked the integration movement in the southern United States, was a student at the Highlander Center.

The Origins of Participatory Literacy Education

THE TERM "participatory literacy education" made its debut in a doctoral dissertation in the late 1980s (Jurmo, 1987). Within a short time, two significant publications on participatory practices in adult literacy and English as a Second Language emerged (Auerbach, 1992; Fingeret & Jurmo, 1989), establishing a foundation for educators and learners to build upon. Over the years, the body of literature on participatory education has slowly expanded (Auerbach, 1996; Campbell, 1994, 1996; Campbell & Burnaby, 2001; Demetrion, 1993; Hayes & Walter, 1995; King, Estes, Fingeret & McCullough, 1993; Norton & Campbell, 1998; Norton & Malicky, 2000; Rodriguez, 2001; Sauve, 2000).

In Canada, Quebec's Francophone literacy educators who work in community-based settings were among the first to emerge as a strong force in the promotion of participatory practices. Quebec's Francophone community-based programs emphasize "collective participation in literacy activities and promote the social, cultural and economic development of the learner" (d'Entremont, 1990, p. 40). These programs also aim "to develop social and political consciousness by developing among the participant learners capacities for critical analysis, choice of actions, and evaluation" (Miller, 1988, p. 17). These programs acknowledge that literacy cannot be reduced to simply learning to read, write, and compute as ends in and of themselves.

In the 1980s, the Francophone literacy community adopted the stance that students should be actively involved in making decisions about the shape and structure of their programs and education. Le regroupement des groupes popularies en alphabetisation du Quebec stated that the student must "be fully involved as a decision-maker in the organization of his or her learning experience" (Miller, 1988, p. 17). This organization and its members believe that literacy can be achieved only by a collective effort in which the individual students play an active role.

In the United States, community-based organizations committed to personal and community development and creating a just society have been leaders in participatory literacy education. During the civil rights movement,

> community organizers ran literacy classes in the South to enable black residents to pass the literacy test that was required in order to become a registered voter. Classes used the voter registration test materials as a key instructional text and involved learners in discussion of human rights and other community issues (Jurmo, 1989, p. 74).

A milestone during the civil rights movement occurred when Congress passed the Voting Rights Act of 1965, making it easier for Southern blacks to register to vote. Literacy tests and other such requirements that tended to restrict black voting become illegal.

Participatory Education Themes

Community

Many scholars and practitioners have begun to appreciate the impact that the development of community and connection have on learners. Scholarship in the area of feminist pedagogy and adult education has emphasized the power and importance of the social role of connection in education settings, not only among learners but between teachers and learners (Sissel, 1996, p. 98).

The building of community is a cornerstone of participatory education. In a world driven by an economic system that stresses individualism and consumerism, there is a longing among individuals to feel connected to others. In struggling to meet the demands of day to day living, students often speak of feeling alone and apart, and wanting an opportunity to share their world with others. Students share a desire for community within their adult literacy programs; they seek a place where people come together to speak, to learn, to reflect, to work, to cooperate, and to help others (Barndt, 2001; Campbell, 1994; Gaber-Katz & Watson, 1991; Malicky, Katz, Norton & Norman, 1997; Sauve, 2000). Community provides a context for "dialogue with others, leading to a recognition of alternative perspectives and insights on experiences and problems" (Taylor & Blunt, 2001, p. 83). Creating such an environment is not always easy, particularly in programs housed in community colleges and school boards and those that emphasize one-to-one tutoring.

The establishment of student groups within volunteer literacy programs is one way to create a sense of community among students[2]. The following quotes are from students who belong to a student group within a volunteer literacy program. These quotes illustrate that as students learn and socialize collectively, they gain a sense of solidarity, which lessens the feelings of isolation (Campbell, 1994, p. 66).

> We're not feeling alone. It's all over the world, [people] have the same problem, you know. [Donna]

> I think just being together with the others, with everybody and talking things out at our meeting…'Cause I know I'm not the only one now, there's other people out there. [Peggy]

> I think just to *be* with them and just to talk how they feel here… and you can share some feelings that others don't understand. [Heidi]

The North American culture tends to value "action, efficiency, getting to 'the bottom line,' often downplaying social interactions in the interests of achieving goals" (Ziegahn, 2001, p. 1). We see this culture reflected in formal, adult academic programs in which educators must adhere to a predetermined set of goals, curriculum, and resources; and students must achieve credits or outcomes in specified subject areas. These programs provide little time for students to engage in social interactions where they can explore the realities of their daily lives. The administrative and material constraints of these programs mean that creating a context where students can participate in an informal exchange of information is often difficult. Behind closed doors, some participatory educators who work in formal adult basic education programs create spaces where students can discuss matters of importance to them. However, community-based and volunteer literacy programs provide the greatest hope for engaging in participatory education and challenging the oppression that results from the isolation and poverty in the students' lives.

Social Relations

The term "community" tends to have positive connotations. It implies fellowship, harmony, unity, and solidarity. The vision of what a community is or can become sometimes overshadows the reality of how a community can exclude people and repress differences. Some educators, as shown in the following statement, have adopted a critical stance towards community:

> It is up to us to make community: to find it, build it, or encourage it to grow in our fragmented world. But can we? Or should we even try, when in spite of good intentions, the effects of community are often more divisive, more exclusive, and more

oppressive, than the absence of community it originally intended to remove? (Godway & Finn, 1994, p. 1)

> **Efforts toward building a community within
> an adult literacy program are not always easy,
> mainly because there are differences among
> students in terms of race, class, gender, sexu-
> al orientation, age, religion, and dis/ability.**

Efforts toward building a community within an adult
literacy program are not always easy, mainly because
there are differences among students in terms of race,
class, gender, sexual orientation, age, religion, and
dis/ability. The ways in which each student processes
information and interprets the word and the world
will depend upon the person's social identity and the
power, privilege, and oppression imbedded within
his/her social identity.

There are many ways in which a student's social identity affects the way
he/she interprets and perceives the world and consequently communicates and
interacts with others. In certain programs students are excluded or silenced
because of their social or cultural identity. For instance, in a classroom where
some students are Mennonite, a woman might remain silent, because Mennonite
men are the spokespeople in their culture. In small northern Canadian communities, Inuit students might be more silent than non-Inuit students. Or, when
young Inuit students and elders are learning together, the younger students
might become silent when the classroom discussion turns towards traditional
topics. Students who were raised in countries with dictatorships might not speak
their minds as they equate silence with safety.

How does one give voice to differences so that students will not be reduced
to exclusion or silence? As educators, how do we begin to form a bridge across
differences among students and between educators and students? One way of
building bridges across differences is to use an activity that will help students
and/or educators reflect on their social identity. I have found that the power
flower activity, described below, invites students to pause and really think about
their identity in relation to others. The activity, which takes approximately 45 to
60 minutes, helps people to identify who they are (and who they aren't) as individuals and as a group, in relation to those who wield power in our society. The
following description is taken from the book *Educating for a Change*.[3]

- Draw the power flower (see Figure 6.1) on a large piece of paper
  and attach it to the wall or floor.

- Introduce the power flower. Explain how the dominant identity is
  the one that wields the most power and authority in society. As a
  group, fill in the dominant social identity of the group on the outside
  petals. For instance, in the gender petal, the dominant social identity
  might be male.

- Distribute a handout of the power flower, and ask people to work in
  pairs. Ask participants to fill in the inner blank petals, and then
  transfer this information to the inner circle of the flower on the wall.

- As a group, reflect upon the information in the flower on the wall and ask:
  - *What is the dominant identity in your community (or workplace)?*
  - *Are you different than the dominant identity? If so, in what way(s)?*
  - *Do you want to share the ways in which this difference affects you?*
  - *How does a particular identity become dominant?*
  - *How does a particular identity become marginalized?*

Figure 6.1 • The power flower

SOURCE: Arnold, R. Burke, B. James, C. Martin, D. & Thomas, B. (1991). *Educating for a change.* Toronto, ON: Between the Lines. Reprinted with permission.

Before the group responds to the last two questions, the term "marginalized" can be discussed. Sheared, McCabe and Umeki (2000) provide a clear and concise description of marginalization. They explain that marginalization

> occurs when one loses power and control over their own lives and over how they (sic) should or believe they ought to live. It is the act of being in the margins while someone else (teachers/educators, program administrators/managers, and policy makers/legislators) is in the center. In 1984, hooks described this phenomenon as being the difference between "living in the center" versus "living in the margins." (p. 167)

After discussing the term "marginalization," the facilitator can provide a concrete example of how a particular identity becomes dominant or marginalized. For instance, gays and lesbians are marginalized because legislation, the Catholic Church, and certain fundamentalist sects tend to support heterosexuality through their laws and policies. First Nations people are marginalized, as they have lost their land, language, and culture through colonization.

You might be thinking that exploring social relations is analogous to walking in a minefield. Certainly, it is challenging work for educators or students, and it is not without its perils. If the diversity of a group is not acknowledged, however, it is highly likely that spoken and unspoken tensions will eventually begin to surface within the group. The naming and acknowledgement of commonalities *and* differences, although difficult, can help to unite a group and create a sense of camaraderie and fellowship (Campbell, 1994; Horsman, 1999).

Efforts to build a community are also difficult when the social relations between educators and students are hierarchical. Within a hierarchical model, there are rigid divisions between the roles of, and the relationships between, students and educators. In contrast, a participatory model transforms the hierarchical structure by involving students in instruction and program management. According to Sissel (1996),

> whether or not a sense of community in the learning setting is created with and among learners and teachers is dependent upon the social dynamics that exist between them. Although social relations between adult educators and learners may appear to be an apolitical phenomenon, the way in which educators speak with and of learners, their modes of interacting with learners, and the choices they make about the act of teaching—when they act either on or with learners—are related to issues of power, privilege, and personal politics. (p. 99)

Participatory education is based on the belief that spaces should be provided for students to express their viewpoints and become involved in making decisions about the shape and structure of their programs. If students are not involved in the decision-making process, the assumptions of educators will be the sole source of information about practice and programming. These assumptions will

> ► Adult literacy is a marginalized sector of the education system. Why and how did this sector of education become marginalized?

determine the content of the lessons and the books purchased for the resource collection.

I can vividly remember a time when my assumptions and those of a colleague proved to be misguided. Although this experience was outside the realm of literacy, it is an excellent example of the importance of representation. In 1991, I volunteered in a storefront ministry based in Flemingdon Park, a low-income, multicultural public housing community in Toronto. The ministry was committed to supporting the residents in their efforts to improve their quality of life and to creating an oasis of peace and safety for those who lived with chaos in their lives.

The minister and I had assumed that the women in the community would appreciate a series of workshops on violence, as many of them were experiencing violence in their lives. Fortunately, we came to our senses and decided to disregard this assumption and engage instead in a participatory process so that the women could voice their issues and concerns about living in Flemingdon Park. We began the process by extending an invitation to the women in the community. The minister and I went door to door, asking women if they would like to attend a meeting to talk about their issues and concerns about Flemingdon Park.

During our first meeting, it became obvious that the women were experiencing extreme social isolation. As young mothers living on social assistance, they were restricted in their ability to travel beyond the boundaries of the community in order to visit friends and family. The women tended not to socialize within the community, mainly because they did not feel safe outside their apartments.

After we had facilitated a process in which the women shared and analyzed their experiences, we moved into the planning for action phase. It was clear that the women did not want workshops on how to deal with violence. Instead, they wanted more lighting on the streets so that they would feel safer at night. They also wanted a neighbourhood wading pool so that the isolation in their lives could be diminished through socialization with other women. This experience was an excellent lesson for me in the importance of representation and not making programming decisions based upon assumptions.

In the field of adult literacy, the term "representation" calls attention to the ways in which adults with low-literacy skills are positioned and represented by the more dominant sectors of society. In a nutshell, representation focuses on *who* is speaking, rather than *what* is being said. Young (1993) asserts that "policy issues are often defined by the assumptions and the priorities of the privileged. [Therefore], specific representation for oppressed groups interrupts this process, because it gives voice to the assumptions and priorities of other groups" (p. 309). Recently, the issue of representation surfaced during a video-teleconference which centred on the topic of measuring student success. The participants included civil servants, researchers, and practitioners. When a civil servant raised the concern that students were not being represented in the discussion, the facilitator could not understand why the students needed to be participants in the discussion. This example gives credence to Young's assertion that oppressed groups are not always invited into the conversation and are, instead, being represented by dominant groups who believe they have the answers and solutions to unresolved issues and problems.

> ▶ Can you think of the ways in which your conscious and unconscious assumptions have impacted your practice?

> Perhaps the first step in establishing egalitarian relations is examining and reflecting upon your power and privilege and the ways in which power and privilege affects (or will affect in the near future) students in your classroom.

Perhaps the first step in establishing egalitarian relations is examining and reflecting upon your power and privilege and the ways in which power and privilege affects (or will affect in the near future) students in your classroom. The impact of privilege can be difficult to understand because "many of us who are privileged have yet to come to the point of seeing that we are" (Godway, 1994, p. 189). Some participatory educators (Auerbach, 2001; Morgan, 2000) use and promote journal writing as a way of critically reflecting upon their practice.

Knowledge

In 1987, Myles Horton and Paulo Freire came together to discuss their experiences with, and thoughts about, education and social change. The following thoughts shared during this conversation, speak to the importance of valuing and honouring students' knowledge.

> Paulo: When the students come, of course, they bring with them, inside of them, in their bodies, in their lives, they bring their hopes, despair, expectations, knowledge, which they got by living, by fighting, by becoming frustrated. Undoubtedly they don't come here empty. They arrive here full of things. In most of the cases, they bring with them opinions about the world, about life. They bring with them their knowledge at the level of common sense, and they have the right to go beyond this level of knowledge. (Horton & Freire, 1990, pp. 156-7)

> Myles: I feel all knowledge should be in the free-trade zone. Your knowledge, my knowledge, everybody's knowledge should be made use of. I think people who refuse to use other people's knowledge are making a big mistake. Those who refuse to share their knowledge with other people are making a great mistake, because we need it all. (Horton & Freire, 1990, p. 235)

Participatory educators believe that the learning process *begins* by sharing the students' experience or knowledge on a particular subject or issue. The following reflections illustrate how students also value opportunities to learn from each other within a social context (Campbell, 1994, p. 65).

> And when it's a group it seems like it's easier to talk about things because what one person is stumped on, the other isn't, and then others come up with different ideas...Like a lot of times, some students just don't know where to go or what to do if they have trouble with, let's say, social assistance, and a lot of

> other students, they've gone through it, and therefore, they know what to do. [Geoffrey]

> I would like to work with other students because I think I could teach them a lot of things...I know what it's like to be a single parent on a fixed income. [Maria]

> We cancelled the parent workshop. Jean said that we could do that here. Like we could come together and talk about the things that we have problems with, and we could talk about it over here instead of going over there. [Heather]

This reflection came from a student who participated in the women's health group at the Learning Centre Literacy Association. When asked, "What can you bring to the group," she responded:

> I know a lot about what women have to go through. Having monthlies, having kids. Dealing with stress. I think I went through just about everything a woman can go through. I have a lot of experience. (Norton & Campbell, 1998, p. 10)

Participatory educators use their facilitation skills with students to make the transition from *sharing* knowledge and experiences within the group to *analyzing* and *extending* this knowledge. Applying an analytical filter to the dialogue serves to move the discussion from the personal to the political. (This notion will be explored further in the section entitled "The Participatory Spiral.") The extension of knowledge is important as there are limits to the body of knowledge that can be constructed by a group of individuals.

One way to connect the *context* or students' experiences to the *text* is to enhance or extend the students' knowledge. When using text, it is important to reinforce the notion that the knowledge in books and other written material does not always represent the "truth"; rather, it represents one point of view or perspective. For instance, texts written by medical doctors and mid-wives hold particular viewpoints about pregnancy and giving birth. These viewpoints are framed by their author's social locations, life experiences, histories, and culture.

Rather than accepting the text at face value, students learn ways to go beyond the surface meaning of a text. Students also begin to see that what "is not said" in a text is just as important as what "is said." As they engage in critical literacy activities, students become critical consumers of the information they read (Duzer & Florez, 1999). When students assume a critical stance or perspective, they are encouraged to examine and question the visible and invisible values and assumptions within text. Students can then link that information to their own experiences, opinions, and biases. Advertisements, which use a combination of visual information and text, are useful tools for introducing and developing critical literacy skills. To create discussion, interest, and critical thinking, students can be divided into small groups or pairs and asked to study advertisements from newspapers and magazines. The following questions encourage students to take a critical stance:

- Who is in this ad?
- Who isn't in this ad? Why?
- What message does this ad send?
- What are the hidden message(s)?
- Does this ad reflect your reality? If not, why not?
- Whose point of view does this ad reflect?
- Who is this ad aimed at or designed to appeal to?
- Are there additional questions that you would like to have answered?

Newspapers can be used to show how texts present particular viewpoints and values. For this activity, newspaper articles that represent different perspectives on social issues are most useful. Since most newspapers are online, keyword searches such as "welfare mothers" or "immigration" can provide instant access to articles that represent different perspectives. As the students read the articles, they can be asked to:

- Identify the "hero" and the "villain."
- Pinpoint emotional language.
- Discuss visible and invisible values.
- Discuss whether the article reflects their experience and knowledge.

The following two articles, from the *National Post* online service, illustrate how the public and private sectors and special interest groups hold different views towards topics and issues, in this case obesity. Using these articles, the educator asks students to share their experiences with trying to eat a healthy diet on a restricted budget. This discussion might lead to questions about why the articles do not address the difficulty of affording nutritious food on a limited income. These articles could also stimulate dialogue on consumer freedom, the medicare system, the role of the state, and individual responsibility. In a participatory context, it is essential to keep in mind that the key responses and conclusions will come from the students themselves. The teacher's principal role is to support, validate, and extend the students' thinking.

Group fights for your right to eat that fatty burger

Coalition opposes growing number of 'health zealots'

J. Scott Orr – May 3, 2002

WASHINGTON – There are groups in Washington lobbying for the environment, endangered species, public health and hundreds of other causes. But who looks out for junk food?

A group called the Center for Consumer Free-dom has taken up the cause. A coalition of more than 30,000 restaurant and tavern owners is standing tall in defence of fattening food. Its motto: "Protecting Personal Responsibility and Protecting Consumer Choice."

The centre, which was set up in 1995, sees itself on the front lines of the battle to defend Americans' right to gorge on artery-clogging burgers, splurge on waistline-expanding doughnuts and guzzle liver-hardening alcohol.

The group has stepped up its efforts, beginning with an advertising blitz on Washington's radio airwaves. It says it fears government meddling in Americans' diets through the imposition of "fat taxes" on foods ranging from fatty meats to sugary treats.

No specific proposals have been presented to Congress, but the centre isn't taking any chances. It plans to spend hundreds of thousands of dollars taking the ads to other cities soon.

"We are a coalition of restaurant and tavern operators allied together to fight the growing movement of food cops and public health zealots, people who want to tell you what to eat and drink and basically how to live your life," said Mike Burita, the communications director.

Fat Canadians imperil health care: McLellan

Mark Kennedy, February 22, 2002

OTTAWA – "Canada is becoming a nation of fat people and the medicare system could become unaffordable unless citizens take more responsibility for their health," says Anne McLellan.

"One of the things that shocked me when I saw the statistics ... was the fact that we are a nation, or becoming a nation, of obese people," the new Health Minister said yesterday,

in her first appearance before a Commons committee to outline her priorities.

Nearly half of Canadian adults are overweight. Ms. McLellan said governments must put more emphasis on convincing people to take charge of their health by losing weight, watching their diet and stopping smoking.

"We have to do more. Otherwise ... it will become very hard

for us to be able to sustain our health care system because the demands upon it will grow," Ms. McLellan said.

If students have received instruction and practice in discerning "Invi-sible Messages," the analysis and response to both articles will provide them with an opportunity to apply this strategy[4].

Participatory Curriculum

A PARTICIPATORY CURRICULUM engages the students' minds, emotions, and spirit, its framework being built upon the students' issues and concerns. Ideally, students and educators work together to develop a framework that not only addresses students' issues, but provides opportunities for them to share, create, analyze, and act upon their knowledge and experiences. A participatory curriculum stands in sharp contrast to a traditional curriculum in which the syllabus is predetermined by a content expert, the lesson plans are developed by the teacher, and the knowledge is transmitted to the students. A participatory curriculum is also different from a learner-centred curriculum in which the lessons are customized to meet the goals of individual students, and the educators are responsive to the student's needs. Figure 6.2 summarizes and compares the three types of curricula.

Figure 6.2 • Types of Curriculum

	PARTICIPATORY Curriculum	LEARNER-CENTRED Curriculum	TRADITIONAL Curriculum
Ideology	Transformational	Liberal	Conservative
Program Goal	Encourage individuals to understand, challenge, and change society.	Encourage individuals to participate more fully in society.	Encourage individuals to function in society as productive citizens.
Content	Contextualized	Individualized	De-contextualized
Lessons	Focus on students' issues.	Focus on student's goals and needs.	Focus on the need to read.
Educator's Role	Problem poser	Facilitator	Problem solver
Student's Role	Active construction of knowledge.	Self-directed learner.	Passive recipient of knowledge.
Power Relations	Transform inequitable power relations.	Ignore power relations.	Reproduce hierarchical power relations.

My first experience with a participatory curriculum development process was at the Learning Centre Literacy Association, a community-based adult literacy and education centre on the periphery of downtown Edmonton. I was contracted to develop a participatory education program on health with a group of female students. The students and I had developed a rapport through working together on a quilt in a craft circle. The health and craft groups were similar in that women shared their experiences; the difference was that the women in the health group "extended their knowledge, and identified steps and support to enhance their health" (Norton & Campbell, 1998, p. 1).

Auerbach (1992) developed a set of principles for participatory curriculum development, and the health program developed at the Learning Centre was an attempt to put these principles into practice. Although students identified issues, their participation in the development and evaluation of the curriculum was limited. As Auerbach has indicated, engaging students in curriculum development is a "slow, gradual process" that involves building trust, the foundation of all candid human communication. The principles developed by Auerbach serve to summarize many of the key ideas put forward in this book, and they lie at the heart of the participatory curriculum:

> Students are engaged in curriculum development at every stage of the process.

Ideally, this means that students participate in identifying issues, generating content, producing materials, determining outcomes, and evaluating learning. This ideal is a slow, gradual process that involves moving back and forth between old and new ways of doing things and making the approach to curriculum itself explicit. Students' increasing participation fosters motivation and self-confidence.

> The classroom is a model: what happens inside the classroom shapes the possibilities outside the classroom.

Both *what* is learned (content) and *how* it is learned (processes) shape students' perceptions of their own possibilities and prepare them for particular ways of acting in the outside world. Classroom social relations are a microcosm of social relations beyond the classroom. Making changes inside the classroom itself models a way of addressing issues and redefining roles outside the classroom.

> The focus is on strengths, not inadequacies.

Students are seen as experts on their own reality, and as such are invited to believe in themselves. The content stresses their capacity to create new knowledge rather than reproduce or duplicate someone else's knowledge. This means investigating, validating and extending what participants can (and want to) do rather than stressing what they can't do or imposing what educators/experts think they should be doing.

> The teacher's role is one of problem-poser rather than problem-solver.

The teacher is not the one with the answers, but the one who facilitates students' discovery of their own answers. The teacher acts as a catalyst for the students' reflection upon their everyday reality. As concerns are identified, the teacher represents them to the class and guides students through an exploration process, contributing linguistic expertise while learning from the students about their reality. The group generates its own ways of addressing concerns through collective dialogue.

> The content comes from the social context.

For literacy to be relevant, what goes on inside the classroom must relate to students' lives outside the classroom; thus, the starting point is the experience of the learner. Students develop literacy by reading, writing, and talking about social factors (like housing, work, or neighbourhood safety) in their family and community contexts and, most importantly, about ways that they can help shape these conditions.

> Content also comes from the immediate context of the classroom.

Because the students' primary shared context is their learning community, negotiating classroom dynamics and procedures is an important part of the content. Transforming these issues into content-based literacy activities, involving students in examining student-teacher roles, making decisions about curriculum content and processes, and resolving conflict, can redefine roles and social relations in the classroom.

> Individual experience is linked to social analysis.

Participants look at their personal situations in light of each other's experiences and examine the root causes of problematic conditions. They talk not only about someone's difficulties in finding an apartment, but about why there is a housing shortage in the first place. This may lead to a discussion about why some landlords prefer to rent to immigrants, while others prefer not to, and ultimately, about strategies they can use for finding housing. This collective reflection depersonalizes problems, provides support, and is the basis for action.

> The content comes from the social context.

The goal is action outside the classroom to address participants' concerns; content is meaningful to the extent that it enables learners to make changes in their lives. This means that reality is not seen as static or immutable; learners can do more than adapt to it. Literacy is not an end in itself, but rather a means for participants to shape reality, accomplishing their own goals. Skills are taught in service of action for change rather than as independent, isolated objectives.

Source: Auerbach, E. (1992). Adapted from Making meaning making change: Participatory curriculum development for adult ESL literacy. *McHenry, Il: Center for Applied Linguistics and Delta Systems. Reprinted with permission, pp. 21-22.*

Putting Principles into Practice: The Difficulties

Many educators have difficulty putting participatory principles into practice because of the learning context in which they are situated. For instance, delivery agencies such as colleges and school boards tend to use traditional curricula, while community-based programs tend to use learner-centred or participatory curricula. This is because, to a large extent, accountability frameworks dictate the type of curriculum used by delivery agencies. Government department(s) that fund institutions usually require statistical information on key performance indicators (KPI) such as the number of students who complete the program, achieve employment, or continue their education. Since funding is contingent on meeting outcomes, institutions are obliged to follow a traditional curriculum that produces results that can be indicated by means of standardized measures.

The primary accountability measure for community-based programs tends to be statistical information about the number of students and tutors who participate throughout the year. Since most community-based programs do not need to provide government funders with results that can be indicated by standardized measures, they can be more flexible in their choice of curriculum. This creates a window of opportunity for using either learner-centred or participatory curricula, or both. The choice of curriculum adopted by community-based programs reflects the political ideology of the delivery agency. Community-based literacy programs that emphasize the "each one, teach one" model tend to promote a learner-centred curriculum. This type of program is usually lodged within a liberal ideology; individuals are encouraged to participate more fully in society in their roles as family members, community members, and workers. Community-based literacy programs that promote a participatory curriculum are designed to address the injustices and inequitable power relations in society. These programs are lodged within a transformational ideology; learning is a collective process where students access community resources and build upon their own knowledge in an effort to understand, challenge, and change society.

The Participatory Spiral

The participatory spiral is a "cyclical model of sharing, analysis, and action in which personal experiences become a springboard for action" (Campbell, 2001, p. 9). Throughout each of the stages of the model[5], participants are encouraged to reflect upon the process (see Figure 6.3). Each stage in the model is described below.

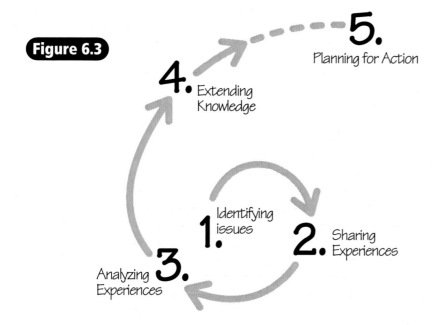

Figure 6.3

5. Planning for Action
4. Extending Knowledge
1. Identifying issues
2. Sharing Experiences
3. Analyzing Experiences

> Identifying Issue(s)

Educators and students work together to identify the students' issues and concerns. By consciously listening to students' conversation during their breaks and informal discussions, educators can identify some of the themes. As students chat with one another and discuss the problems they encounter in their daily lives, the following topics might surface:

- Living on social assistance.
- Raising children.
- Dealing with doctors.
- Finding an apartment.
- Dealing with landlords.
- Looking for work.
- Dealing with addictions.
- Dealing with violence.
- Dealing with learning.
- Dealing with isolation.

A more structured approach to eliciting students' issues involves presenting themes to the students, and asking them to identify issues within each theme. Within the theme of shelter, students might raise complaints about landlords, crowded living conditions, safety, or prostitution. As an example, when I introduced the theme of health to a group of female literacy students, they identified the following topics: stress, learning to say no, exercise, healthy weight, menopause, anger, STDs, living healthy on a low budget, and living with welfare.

> Sharing Experience and Knowledge

Once students and/or educators have identified an issue, they can share and reflect upon their experiences with the issue on hand. Discussions based on personal experiences might be problematic for some educators and certainly raise many questions. This kind of disclosure often gives rise to ethical and moral questions, such as:

- How does listening to personal disclosure "fit" into education? Isn't this therapy? What if a student keeps telling the same story over and over again?
- What if a student shares information that is erroneous, misleading, or libelous?
- To what extent should the educator disclose his/her experiences, feelings, and emotions?
- How does the educator deal with emotion-laden topics?

The answers to these challenges will depend on the situation and context in which they are posed. It is important to note that because participatory education begins with and is situated in the personal, social, cultural, and political lives of students, disclosure is inevitable. As previously noted participatory education deals with and engages minds, emotions, and spirit, its framework being built upon the students' issues and concerns.

> Analyzing Experiences

The transition from sharing to analyzing experience and knowledge is often challenging because there isn't a how-to-manual or an answer key; instead, educators have to "fly by the seat of their pants." For many educators, the key question is, "How does one facilitate a process that connects the personal to the political?" As they listen to one another's stories and identify patterns, students have a way of seeing that their stories are part of a larger political forum, and they have an opportunity to shift their discussion from the personal to the political.

The educator can facilitate a process where students analyze the issue at hand by posing the following questions such as:

- What is the same and what is different about our experiences?
- Why are so many of us experiencing the same problem?
- What are the root causes for the problem?
- What solutions have we tried?

As they identify patterns among their experience, students who view themselves as victims of the system may begin to reposition themselves. Some students might think that because of their problem, they are "bad" parents, employers, or community members. Students may blame themselves for not being able to understand the social assistance system. They might think they are "lousy" parents because they cannot access the services or that they have to lie in order to access the services their children need. When students realize that others are having the same difficulties, they can see that the problem often lies within the system. By applying an analytical filter to their problems, students may begin to see that the problem is not always their fault and they have not done anything wrong.

Moving the discussion from the personal to the political does not necessarily mean that the "personal" is ignored. Quite often, the discussion can be enriched by asking, "To what extent do people bear some or partial responsibility for bringing about positive changes in their lives?"

> Extending Knowledge

Although participatory educators value and honour the students' knowledge, they also know that all knowledge is partial. Students will gain a fuller understanding of issues when they extend their knowledge by accessing information through resource people or written material. As students reach out into the community for information, they might form connections and perhaps alliances with other groups and agencies.

Students begin extending their knowledge when they pose their own questions about the issue they are exploring. The students then work either independently, or in pairs or in small groups, to find answers to the questions by accessing information through libraries, resource collections, the yellow pages, community agencies, and the Internet. The educator contributes by providing the students with tips and techniques for accessing the information they need.

> Planning for Action

As the teacher and students develop a plan for action, the question "What can we do?" is a productive way to enter into this stage of discussion that began with identifying the issue(s). This stage can be frustrating for educators and students, as it often appears overwhelming or impossible for individuals to challenge and change power structures and systems within their community and the larger society. Students can begin to counter their feelings of powerlessness by sharing their experiences with overcoming adversity and standing up for their rights. As they develop personal and group confidence, they can brainstorm ways for dealing with the bureaucracy they typically encounter in the various government systems that control and direct their lives. The overall goal of this process is to empower students so that they have access to the information, resources, and strategies they need to assume control of their lives.

When it comes to planning for action, the question "What counts as change?" often surfaces among educators as many become disheartened and even disillusioned when their efforts do not result in any apparent systemic change. There is one change that I have witnessed time and time again: students move from silence to speech, which is the expression of a movement from object (being powerless) to subject (being powerful). Many participatory educators believe the movement from silence to speech is a prerequisite for systemic change. They contend that in order to be "heard" by those in authority, individuals need to speak their minds. In the following comments, students describe their movement from silence to speech. These comments were recorded during discussion(s) with students who had formed student support groups within their literacy programs. (Campbell, 1994).

> We [the students] all get together, and I wouldn't say anything. If they asked me something, I would just keep quiet and go along with what everybody else was saying and doing. [I] couldn't talk for myself, couldn't even, you know, stand up for myself, like even if I didn't know, I couldn't say, "No, I ain't going to do this." But now, I just about can. [Jean] (p. 68)

> I talk a lot easier now, and I think just being together with the others with everybody and talking things out at our meeting, and that makes it…. I think I've changed a lot. I'm really, I'm more outspoken. [Peggy] (p. 69)

> Students are starting to speak up…I didn't want to join the group because I'm not a very good talker…I don't talk very much sometimes. This is my first time. But now, but now, I'm getting used to it now. Like they say, practice makes speech. [Paul] (p. 69)

> We feel more confident. Some of us used to be so shy we could not even speak to people. [Excerpt from a group interview] (p. 139)

In an ideal world, people know when to speak their minds, when to keep quiet, and when to listen—it's all a question of "balance." As you read earlier, in an adult literacy program, students do not always speak their minds in the classroom, in groups, and in meetings because social positions and power relations inform who speaks and who listens (Campbell, 1996). Students have told me how they are afraid to take a stand or voice their opinion, afraid of saying the wrong thing, afraid to ask questions, and afraid to say "no." Quite often, the students attribute their fear of speech to shyness. hooks (1988) views this shyness as an expression of "deeply embedded, socially constructed restrictions against speech in a culture of domination, a fear of owning one's words, of taking a stand" (p. 17). This fear can emanate from past experiences where, as working class people, they were not heard as they did not speak the dominant language. Participatory practices create a rehearsal ground in which students can learn the dominant language that often excludes them from participating in and speaking up in meetings, in conferences, and in the wider community. One female participant confirmed this notion by saying, "It's maybe kind of good to learn *it* here because, who knows, maybe somewhere down the road you could end up anywhere, even in your work."

The Problem-posing Method

In situations where students are hesitant to bring up personal or social issues that they consider sensitive or a potential source of embarrassment, educators can use the problem-posing method. This method is initiated by using a **code**[6] or prompt that represents the issue. Usually a code can be used to stimulate discussion and explore the students' social reality. A photograph of a house with boarded-up windows might be a suitable code for a group of inner-city residents who are concerned about their living conditions. Codes can also include objects, drawings, posters, skits, videos, role plays, stories, poems, questions, words, and music. The purpose of the code is to provide a stimulus so that students can clearly see the issue or problem, respond to it emotionally, reflect on it critically, and take action to deal with or respond to it. Codes capture the essence of the problem, while representing the issue in an abstract, general sort of way. This tends to depersonalize the problem so that learners can distance themselves from the issue and form generalizations (Auerbach, 1996).

Students have an opportunity to respond to the code, and are then guided through a problem-posing process. This process is similar to the participatory spiral, in that students share and analyze personal experiences, and discuss ways to address and resolve their issues and problems. The following questions can be used to structure the problem-posing process (Auerbach, 1996; Wallerstein, 1983).

Describe the content of the code: *What do you see?*
Who is talking?
What is happening?

Identify the problem represented by the code:	*What is the problem here?*
Relate the problem to the students' experiences:	*Have you experienced this problem? In what ways has your experience been the same? How has it been different? How do you feel about it?*
Discuss the root causes of the problem:	*How has this problem come to be? Why is there a problem?*
Discuss strategies and solutions:	*What have you done in a similar situation? What can we do about this problem?*

In the final stage, "collective action is stressed over individual action because this is often more effective and reinforces collaboration" (Auerbach, 1996, p. 94). In each stage of the process, the questions provide the tools for dialogue.

Participatory education represents a challenging undertaking for educators because there is not a prescribed curriculum. There are no road maps, no blueprints, and no easy answers about how to proceed on a day-to-day process. Instead, educators base their practice on a cyclical model of sharing, analysis, and action in which personal experience becomes a springboard for action. The next section describes the possibilities of teaching reading within a participatory context.

Participatory Education: The Possibilities

IF EDUCATORS VIEW PARTICIPATORY PRACTICES as a vision rather than as a set of goals, and place importance on the process rather than the product, they may be more accepting of the challenges (Campbell, 1994). Educators can sustain their vision of participatory education by considering the possibilities, the opportunities, and the benefits that participatory education offers to educators and students.

- Participatory education creates possibilities for students and educators to come together in a new context—a social context— and as such opens up new ways of being and learning together.

- Participatory education, through the integration of literacy education and social interaction, creates the possibility for a contextualized literacy education that recognizes the collective, social purpose of education.

- Participatory education creates possibilities for challenging the hierarchical social relations that underlie literacy programs and create borders among students, literacy workers, and board members—borders that distinguish '"us" from "them."

- Participatory education creates a rehearsal ground where students can learn the dominant language that often excludes them from participating in the public events and the wider community. Participatory education creates the possibility for students to speak and be heard, and to listen to others from diverse backgrounds.

- Participatory education creates opportunities for literacy workers to examine their own social identity as it relates to that of their students. It presents an opportunity to move beyond descriptors such as "student" and "literacy worker" and to consider how class, gender, and race constitute social identity. By recognizing one's social location and the differences in social identity among people who occupy different subject positions, literacy educators come to acknowledge privilege and unravel its implications in structuring social relations with people who have less privilege.

- Participatory education creates opportunities for students to acknowledge their social and cultural identities in relation to other students in their group and to look at how gender, race, and culture constitute social identity and influence relations with others.

- Participatory education creates opportunities for literacy workers to question their pedagogical approach with students—an approach that rests on social relations as well as on methodology.

- Participatory education integrates the learning of particular skills and strategies through contextualized, purposeful activity. It does not ignore explicit language and literacy development.

Participatory educators continue to engage in participatory education because they believe in community rather than individualism; in students creating personal, social and political knowledge rather than educators transmitting it to them; and in promoting egalitarian social relations rather than hierarchical ones.

CHAPTER SUMMARY

Participatory education creates possibilities for moving beyond constructing knowledge to bringing about change in students' lives and in their communities. The following three themes were woven throughout this chapter:

- **Community:** Participatory education promotes the development of community by combining literacy education with social (inter)action.
- **Social Relations.** Participatory education examines and challenges inequitable power relations within hierarchical structures.
- **Knowledge:** Learning is built around the knowledge that students construct from their social, cultural, and political experiences.

This chapter acknowledged that participatory education is a slow process in which students and educators take small steps towards making positive changes in their lives and their community. For students, this process involves sharing, creating, analyzing, and acting on their knowledge and experiences. For educators, this process involves the following:

- Posing questions rather than seeking answers. When educators seize opportunities to question, discuss, and reflect upon their own practice, they take the first step in developing the awareness that underlies participatory education. Kate Nonesuch (2001), a literacy educator who moderated an on-line discussion about power, stated:

  "More than ever I am aware of the hunger we have as literacy instructors to talk about what we do, although we often feel overwhelmed and stretched nearly to the limit by the needs of our students and the struggle to keep programs afloat and classes working. I value that hunger to talk and to reflect on our practice. I think it is a sign of the health of our profession."

- Examining the issue of representation by asking the question "In this classroom and at this board table, who is speaking for whom?" In other words, are the program and curriculum being shaped by the students' views, issues, interests, and needs? Or, are the program and curriculum being shaped by the educators' conscious and unconscious assumptions?

- Deepening their consciousness about the ways in which power relations within the classroom reflect and perpetuate the inequalities and injustices that students encounter in their daily lives.

I trust that the ideas presented in this book will broaden, deepen, and confirm your understanding of teaching reading to adults. It is my hope, that as you walk away from this book, you will continue to question and reflect upon your practice. As Kate Nonesuch says, "This is the sign of a healthy profession." ❧

References

Arnold, R. Burke, B. James, C. Martin, D. & Thomas, B. (1991). *Educating for a change*. Toronto, ON: Between the Lines.

Auerbach, E. (1992). *Making meaning making change: Participatory curriculum development for adult ESL literacy*. McHenry, Il: Center for Applied Linguistics and Delta Systems.

Auerbach, E. (1996). *Adult ESL/literacy from the community to the community: A guidebook for participatory literacy training*. Mahwah, NJ: Lawrence Erlbaum.

Barndt, D. (2001). Naming, making, and connecting—Reclaiming lost arts: The pedagogical possibilities of photo-story production. In P. Campbell & B. Burnaby (Eds.), *Participatory practices in adult education* (pp. 31-54). Mahwah, NJ: Lawrence Erlbaum.

Campbell, P. (1994). *Participatory literacy practices: Having a voice, having a vote*. Unpublished doctoral dissertation, University of Toronto, Ontario.

Campbell, P. (1996). Participatory literacy practices: Exploring social identity and *relations. Adult Basic Education, 6(3), 127-142*.

Campbell, P. & Burnaby, B. (Eds.) (2001). *Participatory practices in adult education*. Mahwah, NJ: Lawrence Erlbaum.

Cook, G.L. (1987). Educational justice for campmen: Alfred Fitzpatrick and the foundation of Frontier College, 1899-1922. In M.R. Welton (Ed.), *Knowledge for the people: The struggle for adult learning in English-speaking Canada, 1828-72*. (pp. 35-51). Toronto, ON: OISE Press.

Demetrion, G. (1993). Participatory literacy education: A complex phenomenon. *Adult Basic Education, 3(1), 27-50*.

D'Entremont, C. (1990). *The first step: Adult literacy, basic education and academic upgrading for Acadians in Nova Scotia*. Nova Scotia: Department of Advanced Education and Job Training and the National Literacy Secretariat.

Duzer, C.V. & Florez, M.C. (1999). *Critical literacy for adult English language learners*. Washington, DC: National Center for ESL Literacy Education. (ERIC Digest No. EDO-LE-99-07)

Fingeret, A. & Jurmo, P.J. (1989). Participatory Literacy Education. *New Directions for Continuing Education, 42*.

Gaber-Katz, E. & Watson, G.M. (1991). *The land that we dream of: A participatory study of community-based literacy*. Toronto, ON: OISE.

Godway, E.M. (1994). Deconstructing privilege: Reflecting on Audre Lore and Gayatri Chakravorty Spivak. In E.M. Godway & G. Finn (Eds.), *Who is this 'we'?* (pp. 185-197). Montreal, QC: Black Rose Books.

Godway, E.M. & Finn, G. (1994). Introduction: Community: catachresis: community. In E.M. Godway & G. Finn (Eds.) *Who is this 'we'?* (pp. 1-10). Montreal, QC: Black Rose Books.

Hayes, E. & Walter, P.G. (1995). A comparison of small group learning approaches in adult literacy education. *Adult Basic Education 5*(3), 133-151.

hooks, B. (1988). *Talking back: Thinking feminist, thinking black.* Toronto, ON: Between the Lines.

Horsman, J. (1999). *Too scared to learn: Women, violence and education.* Toronto, ON: McGilligan Books.

Horton, M. & Freire, P. (1990). *We make the road by walking: Conversations on education and social change.* Philadelphia, PA: Temple University Press.

Horton, M. Kohl, J. & Kohl, H. (1990*). The long haul: An autobiography.* New York: Doubleday.

Jurmo, P.J. (1987). *Learner participation practices in adult literacy efforts in the United States.* Unpublished doctoral dissertation, University of Massachusetts, Amherst, MA.

Jurmo, P.J. (1989). History in the making: Key players in the creation of participatory alternatives. In A. Fingeret & P. Jurmo (Eds.), *Participatory Literacy Education, New Directions for Continuing Education,* 42, pp. 73-80.

King, J. Estes, J.M. , Fingeret, H. & McCullough, P. (1993). *"It brought a richness to me": A resource manual for participatory literacy practitioners.* Literacy South: Durham, NC.

Krotz, L. Martin, E. & Fernandez, P. (1999). *Frontier College letters: One hundred years of teaching, learning and nation building.* Toronto, ON: Frontier College.

Malicky, G.V., Katz, C. H., Norton, M. & Norman, C.A. (1997). Literacy learning in a community-based program. *Adult Basic Education,* 7(2), 84-103.

Miller, L. (1988). Le Regroupement des groups populaires en alphabetisation du Quebec. *Learning,* 5(1), 16-17.

Morgan, D. (2000). Changing places: A study about factors that can affect sharing the facilitator's roles in a women's writing group. In M. Norton & G. Malicky (Eds.), *Learning about participatory approaches in adult literacy education: Six research in practice studies* (pp. 105-140). Edmonton, AB: Learning at the Centre Press.

Nonesuch, K. (May 7, 2001). *Getting out of the way.* An electronic conference on the e-northwest regional literacy electronic network. Literacy BC: First Class.

Norton, M. & Campbell, P. (1998). *Learning for our health: A resource for participatory literacy and health education.* Edmonton, AB: The Learning Centre Literacy Association.

Norton, M. & Malicky, G. (2000). *Learning about participatory approach in adult literacy education: Six research in practice studies.* Edmonton, AB: Learning at the Centre Press.

Rodriguez, C. (2001). *Educating for change: Community-based/stduent-centred literacy programming with First Nations adults* (Rev. ed.). Victoria, BC: Centre for Curriculum, Transfer and Technology.

Sauve, V. (2000). *Voices and visions: Issues, challenges and alternatives in teaching adult ESL.* Don Mills, ON: Oxford University Press.

Sissel, P.A. (1996). Reflection as vision: Prospects for future literacy programming. In P.A. Sissel (Ed.), *A Community-Based Approach to Literacy Programs: Taking Learners' Lives into Account. New Directions for Continuing Education,* 42, pp. 97-103.

Sheared, V., McCabe, J., & Umeki, D. (2000). Adult literacy and welfare reform: Marginalization, voice, and control. *Education & Urban Society, 32*(2), 167-187.

Taylor, M.C. & Blunt, A. (2001). Situated cognition. *The Canadian Journal for the Study of Adult Education, 15*(2), 79-103.

Wallerstein, N. (1983). *Language and culture in conflict.* Don Mills, ON: Addison-Wesley Publishing.

Young, I.M. (1993). Justice and the politics of difference. In P. Green (Ed.), *Democracy* (pp. 309-316). New Jersey: Humanities Press.

Ziegahn, L. (2001). *Considering culture in the selection of teaching approaches for adults.* Columbus, OH: Center on Education and Training for Employment. (ERIC Digest No. 231)

Notes

1   The "Origins of Participatory Education" is revised and reprinted with permission from Campbell, P. (2001). Introduction. In P. Campbell & B. Burnaby (Eds.), *Participatory practices in adult education* (pp. 1-12). Mahwah, NJ: Lawrence Erlbaum. p. 1-2.

2   Student groups consist of adult literacy students; each student group is responsible for establishing its purpose, based on its needs and interests.

3   Adapted and reprinted with permission from Arnold, R. Burke, B. James, C. Martin, D. & Thomas, B. (1991). *Educating for a change.* Toronto, ON: Between the Lines.

4   The invisible messages technique is described in Chapter Five.

5   The model has been adopted from the spiral model described in Arnold, R. Burke, B. James, C. Martin, D. & Thomas, B. (1991). *Educating for a change.* Toronto, ON: Between the Lines.

6   Paulo Freire coined the term "codification," which is a representation of the learners' day-to-day situations. Wallerstein (1983) changed the term codification to code.

Glossary

Aesthetic reading

The reader's attention is focused on the "lived-through experience of the text" and the thoughts, feelings, images, and associations evoked as the story is read. This response is concerned with the personal nature of the reading experience, rather than with retention of information.

Analytic approach

The analytic phonics approach proceeds from whole to part; that is, a student is presented with a word and is then taught the association of sounds to letters and letter clusters within the word.

Authentic assessment

Authentic assessment uses a wide range of texts and tasks to assess a student's literacy development, skills, processes, and current capabilities. The assessment tasks include interviews, **informal reading inventories**, miscue analysis, **retellings**, dialogue and response journals, checklists of learner goals, self-assessments, and **portfolio assessment**.

Automaticity

Automaticity is the ability to recognize words instantly. The automatic recognition of words enables the reader to shift his/her primary processing efforts from word identification to the construction of meaning.

Bias

Bias occurs in testing when items systematically measure differently for different ethnic, gender, or age groups. Test developers reduce bias by analyzing items separately for each group, then identifying and discarding items that appear to be biased.

Bottom-up theory

According to this theory, also known as the "text-based" model, reading is primarily depicted as a perceptual process—the reader processes the information in the text by proceeding from part to whole. The assumption underlying this part-to-whole approach is that learning to read is easier if you start with small, separate pieces of information. Bottom-up theorists believe that individuals learn to read by progressing through a linear, sequential series of skills.

Cloze procedure

This is an instructional strategy that encourages students to use meaning and syntactic cues to restore deleted words from a piece of text.

Code

"A code sums up or 'codifies' into one statement a problem (or contradiction) that people recognize in their lives: need for English vs. need for work, disappointment vs hope from expectations in the U.S" (Wallerstein, 1983, p. 19).

Content validity

Content validity is concerned with the extent to which a test is an adequate sample of the attribute, trait, or skill assessed. The test items are generally used to evaluate the validity of the test.

Contextualized skills instruction

Authentic reading and writing activities are used to teach skills.

Deductive instruction

Deductive instruction occurs when the educator presents knowledge to students, who then use that knowledge in new situations. This type of instruction is based on a transmission model of knowledge.

Directed Reading Thinking Activity (DRTA)

DRTA is a step-by-step instructional activity that encourages readers to use their background knowledge to predict what might happen in a story and to use cues from the text to evaluate and revise these predictions.

Expository text

This is a form of writing that provides information, detailed explanations, judgements, and supporting examples (Bainbridge & Malicky, 2000).

Efferent reading

In the efferent stance, the reader's attention is focused on information to be retained after the reading.

Frustration level

This is level at which a student experiences difficulties in word recognition and/or comprehension. A student who is reading at his/her frustration level has poor comprehension (below 70 percent) and/or word recognition (90 percent or below).

Fry readability graph

This is a method of estimating the difficulty level of written text.

Graphophonic cues

The graphophonic system refers to letters and sounds; when using this system, the reader analyzes the print cues in the text and makes predictions that are visually similar to the text

Herringbone technique

This instructional strategy is aimed at directing the student's attention to specific key details in the text. The Herringbone form provides a structure that assists students in attending to and remembering the text information.

Incidental skills instruction

Skills are taught in mini-lessons when they are needed.

Inductive instruction

Students are presented with specific facts; and through the process of investigation, they build generalizations about the facts. This model is aligned with social constructivism.

Inference questions

This type of question requires the readers to formulate a response by relying on their background knowledge *and* information from the text.

Informal reading inventory

An informal reading inventory is an individually administered diagnostic instrument that allows the instructor to make structured observations of the reader's oral and silent reading performance.

Instructional Level

The level at which a student reads with adequate comprehension and word recognition. A student who is reading at his/her instructional reading level has good comprehension (70-90 percent) and word recognition (91-98 percent), but would still benefit from some instruction in these areas.

Interactive reading theory

This theory views reading as primarily a cognitive process, and information processing proceeds from whole to part and part to whole (Rumelhart, 1977). The interactive theory of reading rests on two assumptions about language, thinking, and learners (Lipson & Wixson, 1997). The first assumption is that reading is an active process of constructing meaning that occurs as the reader interacts with the text in a particular context or situation. The second assumption is that readers use three language-cueing systems—graphophonic, syntactic, and semantic—as they construct meaning.

Isolated skills instruction

Reading instruction is decontextualized; students are presented with isolated words and tasks.

K-W-L

K-W-L is an instructional strategy. It provides a framework to elicit readers' background knowledge and interest prior to their reading expository text, in order to establish a purpose for reading and help readers reflect upon their reading (Ogle, 1986).

Language experience

Language experience is an integrated writing-reading-discussing activity in which the instructor records a dictated story or personal anecdote from a student or group of students.

Language experience stories provide the student with familiar and meaningful text that is highly predictable and easy to read.

Literacy event

A literacy event is an activity that usually involves written text and spoken language (Barton & Hamilton, 2000). Literacy events are situated in different domains, such as the home, the school, the workplace, and the community.

Matrix

A matrix or rubric contains specific sets of criteria that clearly define for both student and educator a range of acceptable and unacceptable performance.

Miscue

Kenneth Goodman (1969) concluded that the "errors" struggling readers make were really not errors at all. He observed that in their attempts to decode new or unfamiliar words, they were using language cueing systems inappropriately and thus, unproductively. He suggested that rather than making errors, these readers were "mis-cueing," and aptly termed their attempts "miscues."

Miscue analysis

Miscue analysis is a systematic examination of the student's miscues. It can reveal the reader's current capabilities to use language cueing systems; and can also provide the foundation for a successful intervention or instructional program that responds to the reader's needs.

Norm group

A group of subjects of knowledge demographic characteristics (age, gender, etc.) to whom an individual's performance can be compared.

Oral retelling

A retelling occurs when a student reads a piece of text and then retells the text in his/her own words. A retelling is sometimes referred to as an "unaided recall."

Participatory education

Participatory education is a collective effort in which the participants are committed to building a just society through individual and socioeconomic transformation, and ending domination through changing power relations. As educators and students work towards building a just society, participants share, create, analyze, and act on their knowledge and experiences (Campbell, 2001).

Portfolio assessment

Portfolio assessment is a collection of a learner's work over time. This work includes book reports, responses to literature, checklists of writing/reading progress, journals, reading logs, and demonstrations of reading performance, etc.

Reliability

Reliability refers to the degree to which test scores are consistent over time and different test situations.

ReQuest procedure

This instructional activity is designed to encourage students to formulate their own questions about the material they are reading, in order to attend to and process text more carefully.

Retelling

A retelling occurs when a student reads a piece of text, and then retells the text in his/her own words. A retelling is sometimes referred to as an "unaided recall."

Schema theory

Schema theory is an explanation of how people store their knowledge, how they learn, and how they remember what they have learned (Anderson & Pearson, 1984). This theory suggests that knowledge is stored in memory and packaged in units called schemata.

Semantic cues

The semantic system refers to meaning; when using this system, the reader analyzes meaning cues and makes predictions about unfamiliar words that "make sense."

Social constructive theory

Proponents of social constructivism define reading as the active construction of meaning from cues in the text and from the reader's background knowledge within a social context (Bainbridge & Malicky, 2000). This theory emphasizes the social construction of knowledge and meaning: what we think and what we know is viewed as a result of social experiences and interactions. Specifically, one's knowledge and ideas are related to cultural identity and shaped by ethnicity, primary language, gender, and social class.

Syntactic cues

The syntactic system, commonly known as grammar, refers to the structure or word order of sentences; when using this system, the reader analyzes syntactic or grammatical cues and makes predictions about unfamiliar words that "sound right."

Synthetic phonics approach

In the synthetic approach, the student is taught the sounds that are associated with individual letters or letter clusters. The student is then taught how to blend the sounds to form words.

Systematic skills instruction

Skills are taught sequentially in a systematic set of planned lessons.

Think-aloud strategy

This strategy utilizes the modelling process. The teacher verbalizes his/her own thoughts while reading a passage orally so that students will realize how and when to do the same. As the passage is read, the students read the same passage silently and listen to the teacher's self-commentary.

Top-down theory

According to this theory, reading is primarily a language-thinking or psycholinguistic process, with information processing proceeding from whole to part. This theory is based on the assumption that readers use their knowledge about language and the world to form hypotheses about the meaning of texts (Smith, 1973).

Validity

Validity is the extent to which a test measures what is authors or users claim it measures. Test validity is concerned with the accuracy of the inferences that can be made on the basis of test results.

About the Author

Pat Campbell began working in literacy in 1981, teaching high school English in Nigeria under the auspices of CUSO. Since 1985, Pat has worked within the field of adult literacy as a program coordinator, software and curriculum developer, researcher, writer, trainer, consultant, and sessional instructor at the University of Alberta. She is the co-author of several publications, including *Participatory Practices in Adult Education*, *Canadian Adult Reading Assessment* and *The Adult Diagnostic Reading Inventory.* ❧